CALLED TO QUESTION

CALLED TO QUESTION

A Spiritual Memoir

Joan D. Chittister, OSB

SHEED & WARD
Lanham • Chicago • New York • Toronto • Oxford

In reverent remembrance
of Theophane
who never feared to question
and so had better answers
than most.

Published by Sheed & Ward
An imprint of Rowman & Littlefield Publishers, Inc.
A wholly owned subsidary of The Rowman & Littlefield Publishing Group, Inc.
4501 Forbes Boulevard, Suite 200
Lanham, MD 20706

PO Box 317
Oxford
OX2 9RU, UK

Distributed by National Book Network

The journal that Sr. Joan Chittister refers to in *Called to Question* is from *In Good Company: A Woman's Journal for Spiritual Reflection* published by Pilgrim Press, 1998.

Copyright © 2004 by Joan D. Chittister, OSB

British Library Cataloguing in Publication Information Available

Library of Congress Cataloging-in-Publication Data

Chittister, Joan.
  Called to question : a spiritual memoir / Joan Chittister.
    p. cm.
  Includes bibliographical references.
  ISBN 1–58051–143–0 (alk. paper)
  1. Spiritual life—Catholic Church. 2. Chittister, Joan. I. Title.
BX2350.65 .C48 2004
271' .97—dc22

                                                      2003022428

Printed in the United States of America

∞™ The paper used in this publication meets the minimum requirements of American National Standard for Information Sciences—Permanence of Paper for Printed Library Materials, ANSI/NISO Z39.48-1992.

CONTENTS

**Immersion in Life:
The Other Side of Inwardness
97**

**Resistance:
The Gospel Imperative
125**

CONTENTS

Acknowledgments

"ONCE UPON A TIME," THE STORY GOES, A SEEKER ASKED a monastic, "What do you do in a monastery?" And the old monastic said, "Oh, we fall and we get up, and we fall and we get up, and we fall and we get up again." The story tells a poignant tale about the difference between faith and despair, between perfectionism and human development. It's a story about growth. It's an indicator of the sanctifying nature of mistakes and miscalculations. It's a signal of the misunderstandings that grow up in every generation about what life and spirituality are really all about.

This book traces both the falling and the getting up process that takes us all into the center of ourselves to find the reason and the strength to bother going on when we fail so often.

It is a discouraging process sometimes to need to begin over and over again to complete the process of spiritual growth, which we tend to believe should be linear when it is, in fact, circular to the core. It's also an embarrassing process in a world that likes to think of "progress" in degrees of advancement rather than in measures of depth.

It is, at the same time, an exhilarating process this coming to awareness of the life within and the God within that life. It is the discovery of the freedom that comes with beginning again, with finding new truth, new ways of being alive, new moral standards that are broader and deeper and more liberating than any amount of disciplines or rituals or negative asceticisms can ever be.

This is a book that examines the multiple threads that make up the lifelong warp and woof of the spiritual experience. It gives no single set of rules. It describes no mystical secrets. It guarantees no certain system of spiritual advancement. It simply looks at all the dimensions of life as we live it today and asks what, if anything, is holy-making about any of it.

It asks whether life as we know it has anything to do with life as ancient spiritual writers declared it to be good.

It is, in other words, an excursion into the questions and soul-searching of one person but it is not, if it is true, only one person's story. It is every person's story. Yours as well as mine. And it is not traveled alone, this path to purpose and perception. It happens in conjunction with all the experiences and truths of all the rest of all the people of my world.

To test that concept, I asked a number of people— Ann Halloran, Anita Banas, John Perito, Gail Grossman Freyne, Daniel Gomaz, Virginia Swisher, Sandra DeGroot, Kathleen Stephens, Thomas Bezanson, Mary Ann Reese, Maureen Tobin, Mary Lou Kownacki, Marlene Bertke, Mary Miller, Anne McCarthy, Ellen Porter, and Linda Romey— to read the text with these concerns in mind: Do you recognize these questions? Do you own the answers? Do you honor the truth of them?

I am forever grateful to the honesty, the insights, and the outpouring of personal experiences prompted by my own. These readers gave breadth and depth to what would otherwise be simply the meanderings of one person's otherwise totally disconnected experience. That is no small hallmark or proof that we all share the same human condition and so we can all hope to come through the questions of life sound and sane and maybe even spiritual.

I'm grateful, too, for Mary Lou Kownacki and Jeremy Langford, my editors, who recognized that I had pressed beyond a book on the history of spirituality to the ways of spirituality itself. Finally, I am grateful to the staff around me—Maureen Tobin, Mary Grace Hanes, and Susan Doubet—who continue to make my writing possible and keep the rest of my life sound, sensible, and somewhat mentally healthy while I do.

This book ends nothing. My one hope is that it will begin in others the process that it reflects in me. All the uncertainty, all the confusion, all the waiting for life to clarify and the spirit to grow are more than worth it.

Finally, I'm grateful to Theophane Seigel, OSB, long-ago mentor and model, who showed me that life was more about questions than it was about answers, more about seeking than simply about dying in the dry smugness of questionable certainties. She taught me to do what today demanded, knowing that to be truly mature, truly spiritual people, we had to be about the development of better insights for tomorrow.

PROLOGUE:
THE JOURNEY FROM
RELIGION TO SPIRITUALITY

*The things of the soul must always be considered as plentiful,
spacious and large.*

—Teresa of Avila

*But what are "the things of the soul"? Surely they are every breath
we breathe, every word we hear, every thought we think. The things
of the soul have been too long compartmentalized. And so we got religion but not spirituality. We got church but not God. We got the
sacred but not the sacredness of the secular. Or better yet, the revelation that there is nothing "secular" at all.*

—Joan Chittister, Journal, September 9

IF THERE IS ONE THING THAT WE HAVE ALL BEEN TAUGHT
to fear, it is surely questions. There are some things, we learn
early, that are never to be challenged. They simply are. They
are absolute. They come out of a fountain of eternal truth.
And they are true because someone else said they are true.
So we live with someone else's answers for a long time. Until the answers run dry. I know that because I myself have
been caught in the desert of doubt and found the answers to
be worse than the questions could ever be.

I had one cousin who got divorced, for instance, another one who—I learned the word later—was gay, a third
who had long ago simply ceased to have anything to do with
religion, and a fourth who had married out of the church.
My grandmother prayed for all of them and disowned none
of them. "God understands us," she said to no one in particular when their names came up in family gatherings.
Grandma herself, I was sure, was very holy, but I wondered
about that kind of thinking. After all, all of those things
were wrong. Everyone knew that.

Then one day, after years of training in all of the religious certitudes of the time, I ran headlong into a situation that led me to realize that the spiritual life is not at all as clear as the books had led me to believe.

I remember the incident with startling clarity. I found myself at a conference in Rome with a roomful of delegates from religious orders from all over the world. The women were concerned about the fact that Rome had published a document making daily Mass and Eucharist an "essential element," a requirement, of religious life in all the convents of the world. But most religious orders—and many parishes, as well, by that time—had no access to priests, a delegate told the cardinal. Daily Eucharist was simply not possible anymore, the others all agreed. Since everyone knew that, they wondered, why require it?

The cardinal's answer brought me up short. "If you are unable to receive the Eucharist itself," he said to us over and over again, "then you must teach the sisters the Eucharist of Desire." But what's the use of that, the women challenged him, if having daily Eucharist is impossible anyway? "Because," the cardinal insisted with some degree of irritation, "if you desire the Eucharist, you have the Eucharist!"

His priest assistant, realizing that the women were still troubled by the answer, still sure the cardinal had not understood them, still incredulous at the response, leaned forward to clarify the situation. "What the cardinal is saying, Sisters," he spelled out patiently and slowly, "is that it is not the Eucharist you lack. What you lack is simply the priestly presence." The silence in the room spoke a language of its own. I shook my head in disbelief. Apparently, we had been getting up at six o'clock in the morning every morning of our lives more for the presence of the priest than for the presence of Jesus. What was really real here?

I learned the lesson of my life that day. Obviously, there is a point at which the old answers cease to work. Obviously, there is a point at which the spiritual life becomes a person's own responsibility. Then, we discover, answers are cheap. Everything we have been so certain about for years becomes less and less certain every day. We find ourselves at a spiritual crossroads. Is there anything here worth believing, anything here worth pursuing? And if so, what and why?

It is the moment when we start to go back over all the questions, to look again at all the rules, to begin for the first time to examine the originating circumstances that underlie all the laws. We look at all the absolutes, and we begin to question them. One at a time; incident by incident; issue by issue: we question them all.

What we had once feared even to wonder about, we begin to dissect one idea at a time. Some ideas we come to suspect. Others we come to doubt.

That day, I realized when I looked back later—the day I heard that I could have the Eucharist without having it, but had to go to it, nevertheless, when a priest was there—was the day I began the conscious, perilous, journey from religion to spirituality, from the certainties of dogma to that long, slow, personal journey into God. That day I began my own wrestling match with God, which no catechism, no creed, could mediate. From then on, I realized, I would have to dare to ask the questions no one had ever wanted me to ask.

Most of all, I began to listen for clues to the ways other people negotiated the tension between the necessary questions and the institutional answers that lay tangled in every spiritual life. I listened to understand how other people stayed on the path they were on once they discovered that they were no longer sure of either the way or the end of it.

I listened to Buddhist monks and Sufi masters, to reformers and mystics, to nuns and mothers, to women as well as to men. I listened to my mail. One after another, people wrote to me about leaving their churches, finding God, questioning their own spiritual worth.

As a result, over time, I've come to a new awareness: I am not the only person who has gone through life watching as one certainty after another is dismantled and turns to dust. Nor am I alone in the realization that there is another kind of certainty that grows stronger in us every day as we begin to make a new spiritual vessel out of the shards of the old one. I began to trust the questions themselves to lead me beyond answers to understanding, beyond practice to faith. I knew with crystal clarity one thing and one thing only: There is such a thing as a spiritual life that is deeper—and truer to the demands of the world around it—than simply the routines of religious discipline, and I wanted it.

So I began to write my ideas down. I began to use my questions themselves to chart my way through the dark waters of a life I found to be not always navigable by given standards. I began to keep a spiritual journal. And it is that journal that is the basis for this book.

This journal was never meant to be a diary—and it is not. In the first place, it was written over a period of almost five years. It is not a daily record of anything. In the second place, there is nothing in it about people or circumstances or the events of the day. It is simply a record of ideas and their implications for the spiritual life today. To be specific, it is a record of the way my ideas played off of other people's ideas whose thoughts are, therefore, also recorded here.

This book began in a daybook that had been constructed around various quotations from a selection of spiritual writers. I made my entries a kind of dialogue with the idea of the day as I saw it in my own life at that particular moment.

These comments on the ideas of spiritual writers whose works cross multiple traditions became grist for the understanding of my own life. They are not an exploration of what a particular statement might say about the writers of the quotations themselves. On the contrary, they have to do with whatever my own questions were at the time. They go beyond the fear of being wrong to the freedom to be honest enough to see life as it is, rather than the way we are told it is supposed to be.

This journal of spiritual quotations became free space where my soul could see the light of day and inhale the fresh air of the search in companionship with others who had dealt with the same kind of questions, the same kind of hopes, I had. It stretched my thinking beyond myself, but it also exposed me to myself, raw and searching.

It was a dubious venture, this willingness to write down in raw form what I myself grappled with in the spiritual life. After all, if I were really going to explore the currents within me, if I were really going to be honest with myself, there was no room for subterfuge here, no need for nuances, no time for subtleties. I was, after all, writing to me.

More than dubious, however, it could also be a reckless undertaking. What if anyone ever read the ideas I would so honestly write? What if they realized how unclear I was about some things, how much I had struggled with others? What if they read my questions and were shocked that anyone would ask such questions at all? What if they read it and considered it a silly waste of time, a kind of fruitless pretension—as in, Who cares? Then, I would be embarrassed by my very existence.

One of the items in the journal put the whole matter quite starkly. Thaisa Frank and Dorothy Wall wrote, "Writing is an audacious act to begin with." And I replied,

> Writing makes a person very vulnerable. It opens you to public criticism, to ridicule, to rejection. But it also opens conversation and thought. It stirs minds, and touches hearts. It brings us into contact with our souls. So how can it possibly be a waste of time, an idle act, a mistake, a betrayal of truth? Who can possibly tell us not to do it?

But they do. Institutions silence and suppress thought regularly. Governments jail dissenters. Churches excommunicate them. Corporations fire them. Communities shun them. But tomorrow's great new insight is always yesterday's foolish idea. I decided to risk a few ideas of my own. Ideas are the coin of the spiritual realm. They are the price of admission to the spiritual life. They lead us beyond ourselves to the Great Idea that makes all of life worthwhile.

When I began this project, I had intended to write a book on spirituality—an introduction to spirituality, if you will—as if, perhaps, spirituality were a product that could be categorized, packaged, and sold. The more I tried to write it, the less I cared about it. That book, I knew, had already been well done by others more prepared than I to trace and explain the history of each period or school of spirituality. I was more concerned, on the other hand, with what is happening now to influence the spirituality of this crossover moment in time. I was looking for another approach to spirituality.

I decided to look at the spiritual questions and life issues that plague us on a daily level—however mundane, however troublesome—rather than look at the great sweeping topics that have come to define our spiritual history: the nature of Jesus, the means of redemption, the modes of revelation. I began to realize that, in the end, we are each and all of us the real subject matter of the spiritual life.

It's possible, of course, to wend our way through life superficially, questioning nothing and calling that faith. Or we can choose to look ourselves in the center of our souls, admit the worst, whatever the pain of that, and pursue the best, even when we are totally unsure where that pursuit will take us. This book is an attempt to be true to the struggle to create for ourselves a spirituality that comes out of both the essentials and the uncertainties of life, rather than its pieties.

"God is gracious and merciful," the journal reminded me, "slow to anger and abounding in steadfast love." But I wrote back to it,

> Who is this God, really? Who is this God whom we have fashioned out of the light of our needs and the hopes of our hearts? When we are vengeful, we tell tall tales of an angry God. When we are sick with our own sin, we find ourselves a God of mercy. When we are pressed down, face in the sand, we know what a God of Justice is all about? Is this God? Or is God the measure of how deep our smallness goes, how great our parching thirst for love? Surely God is all of this. And more. The more we cannot in our smallness and our thirst even begin to imagine.

This book looks at the common questions or dimensions of life as we know them in our daily lives—not answers as we've been given them—in an attempt to unravel their many meanings, to give them flesh, to honor their spiritual import now and here, in our time and in our own lives.

This is a book about spirituality, not about religion, however important religion may surely be to the development of spirituality. It is not a book about theory or history or systematic theology. It is a book about the spiritual issues that have emerged in my own life and, perhaps, even in yours. The only difference between your spiritual broodings and mine may be that I have written mine down—in all their simplicity, in all their uncomfortable plainness. Writing is the way I think things through. If it can serve others as a mirror for their own spiritual insights and concerns, so much the better. "Writing . . . is a form of listening, helping me discover what's wrong . . . in my world as well as what delights me," Susan G. Wooldridge wrote. And I said to that,

> Right: I spend so much time trying to be "objective" but it is all a sham. I cannot be disinterested in the sexism and cruelty, the authoritarianism and legalisms that purport to be of God.

This book is not objective. It is a personal excursion through questions that for years I feared to ask because they had all been answered. Now I am convinced that not to answer them for ourselves means that we will fail in the only thing that, in the end, the spiritual life is surely all about—the search for meaning and for life.

We suckle ourselves on clear or comfortable answers because we fear to ask the questions that make the real difference to the quality and content of our souls. The spiritual life begins when we discover that we can only become spiritual adults when we go beyond the answers, beyond the fear of uncertainty, to that great encompassing mystery of life that is God.

Chapter One

RELIGION:
A FINGER POINTING AT THE MOON

I'm being prodded into a new piece of soul work. What would it mean to live, welcoming all?

—Sue Monk Kidd

Sue Monk Kidd comes from the same place I do—from a theological ghetto. The only difference is that hers was Baptist and mine was Roman Catholic. Each of us, every tradition, has to some extent been arrogant, exclusive, and controlling. Now two women like ourselves have found God outside the denominational pale as well as in our own churches. That's dangerous—both for the denomination and for us. But for me, at least, there is no going back to any totalitarianism that calls itself religion.

—Joan Chittister, Journal, June 15

I WAS AN IRISH CATHOLIC CHILD OF A ROMAN CATHOLIC mother and a Presbyterian stepfather. A "mixed marriage," they called it euphemistically. What they meant was that we were right and he was wrong. We had the truth, and he did not. We had faith, and he did not. We would go to heaven. He? Well, heaven, for him—for them, for *Protestants*, I had come to understand—was at best uncertain. Sad, I knew, but true, nevertheless. Except that down deep in me, even then, the justice of that statement went begging.

The problem revolved around the fact that my step-father was a good man. He was honest and hardworking and unpretentious. He'd even earned a Bible for perfect attendance at Sunday school. Who was this God, then, who would burn the good and the believing like him because, though they kept the same rules, they kept them differently? I forced the question down deep inside of me. It could not be spoken out loud. Its answer was not to be quibbled with. But the question stayed with me all my life. That question and many another like it.

And so religion became the center of my life. I haunted churches the way other children haunted back alleys and open hillsides and high grass and dark cellars. I went from church to church, smelling the cool, damp air of their high vaulted caverns. I lit candles in every candlestand along the way. Then I dropped to my knees at the marble altar rails next to each flickering bank of flames to draw God's attention to the petition they represented. Most of all, I studied my catechism. Correction: No, I did not "study" it. In the manner of Catholic children everywhere, I swallowed it whole. I memorized every word of it. I knew all the rules. I could recount every feast day. I could recite every gift of the Holy Spirit. I could list every capital sin.

And yet, some of them already didn't count for me. We were, after all, in the kind of marriage that was itself outside the norm. Besides that, my mother didn't go to Mass, the most serious problem of them all. And when we took our annual summer trip to the Chittister homestead for family functions, I went to Sunday school classes with my Protestant cousins. I knew early on that life was not really the way the church said it was. But I never questioned the value, the absolute certainty, of the laws themselves.

Nevertheless, years later, I wrote a passage in my journal that said I had come light-years away from that kind of intellectual submission, that kind of fierce unquestioning. "The teaching was," I knew; "Father said," I realized; "Sister taught," yes. But I had clearly gone on parsing dictums, regardless, because experience itself challenged all the absolutes they taught me. It wasn't that I was only now coming to understand things. The fact is that at some level I had always understood them differently, but never said so. "The soul is capable of much more than we can imagine," the journal quoted Teresa of Avila as saying. And I wrote in return,

> I believe so much in the breadth of the soul that every day I respect less and less those things in religion—in church—that bind it. We tie the soul down, we nail it to the canons, we snuff it in midflight. We stop it from seeking the God who is greater than the Platonists, broader than the antimodernists, more full of life than the Jansenists. God save us from the smallness we practice in the name of religion.

The problem of the nature of faith plagues us all our lives. Is openness to other ideas infidelity, or is it the beginning of spiritual maturity? What is it that can possibly take us so far afield from the initial believing self? How do we explain to ourselves the journey of getting from there to here, from unquestioning adherence to institutional answers, to the point of asking faithful questions? It took years before I realized that maybe it is belief itself, if it is real, that carries us there. Maybe if we really believe about God what we say we believe, there comes a time when we have to go beyond the parochialisms of law. Maybe, if we are to be really spiritual people, we can't afford the mind-binding of denominationalism. In order to find the God of life in all of life, maybe we have to be willing to open ourselves to the part of it that lies outside the circles of our tiny little worlds.

The Sufi tell of disciples who, when the death of their master was clearly imminent, became totally bereft. "If you leave us, Master," they pleaded, "how will we know what to do?" And the master replied, "I am nothing but a finger pointing at the moon. Perhaps when I am gone you will see the moon." The meaning is clear: It is God that religion must be about, not itself. When religion makes itself God, it ceases to be religion.

But when religion becomes the bridge that leads to God, it stretches us to live to the limits of human possibility. It requires us to be everything we can possibly be: kind, generous, honest, loving, compassionate, just. It defines the standards of the human condition. It sets the parameters within which we direct our institutions. It provides the basis for the ethics that guide our human relationships. It sets out to enable us to be fully human, human beings.

Clearly, religion is much more than dogmatism. And thank God for that, because dogmatism would not take religion very far at all.

Every time dogmatism reigns, in fact, religion is diminished. When a religion knows when the end of the world will come, and the date passes without incident, that religion fails itself. When religion decrees salvation for some, for our kind, and moral disaster for the rest of humankind—and that in the face of the goodness we see everywhere in every people on earth—it betrays the very God of love it teaches. When religion divides peoples on the basis of spiritual superiority, rather than unites them as common creatures of a common God, it rends the garment of humanity. It gives the lie to the God of cosmic creation. Hildegard of Bingen, my journal reminded me, wrote, "Just as a circle embraces all that is within it, so does the Godhead embrace all." And I wrote in response,

> It is this awareness of the universal God that we miss in life. Our God has always been a Catholic God—or at very least a Christian God. We have, as a result, missed so much of God's revelation. So I fail to find God in the rest of the world. That makes other people so easy to kill . . . Indians, Arabs, Jews, and Asians don't have much of a chance when our God wants their God eradicated.

Indeed, religion at its worst is a sham. But religion at its best anchors us to the best in ourselves, as well.

Religion at its best gives substance to life. Most of all, it enables us to find meaning in life. It gives purpose to the human condition. It sets the human compass toward home. It requires us to be more than we ever thought we could become. It raises our sights beyond ourselves. It sets standards for us that are above the lowest level of the self.

In becoming religious creatures, we become creatures who accept the limitations of creaturehood. Religion teaches us that only God is God. And we are not it. When we learn to recognize the inherent restraints of our own humanity, we can make room for the rest of the world. And so the world is saved from our insufferable sense of superiority.

But religion also gives us reason to hope that God's goodness will make up for what is lacking in us. When we are weak, God is our strength. When we are abandoned, God is with us. And so, we grow to be people who can prevail against despair. We find ourselves with faith not only in God, but in the essential value of life itself.

Religion, this great treasure-house of the faith, is the history of our family heroes. It presents us with an historic stream of witnesses from every people on earth who chose the holy, in the face of rejection and ridicule, whatever the cost to themselves. They dared courage, rather than cooperation with evil. They chose love, rather than law. They stood for justice, rather than self-interest. They sought the transcendent, rather than the immediate.

We walk in line with those, religion reminds us, who gave themselves for the great things of God. Doubters themselves perhaps, thinkers always, they clung to a faith beyond the institution itself, beyond the "answers," because there is a place, they knew, where answers end. And it is religion that taught them that.

At the same time, no doubt about it, religion is often religion's own worst enemy. The tension between religion at its best and religion at its worst drives people from church to church, searching for authenticity. It drives them, as well, from the God of the institution to the God of the spirit within. When religion makes itself God, when religion gets between the soul and God, when religion demands what the spirit deplores—a division of peoples, diminishment of the self, and closed-mindedness—religion becomes the problem.

Then, spirituality is the only valid answer to the cry of the soul for the kind of life that makes life possible.

Chapter Two

SPIRITUALITY:
BEYOND THE BOUNDARIES OF RELIGION

Great delight in God overwhelms me.

—Margaret Ebner

*Delight in the God I have found to be within gives me the strength
to hold out against any Church and its heresies about God, about
women, about ordination. The God within is a raging cry in me.
And no other voice is strong enough to drown it out. It is the only
voice I have heard for years.*

—Joan Chittister, Journal, May 27

"BASILICA," THE ENGLISH WORD FOR THOSE GREAT,
massive, ponderous buildings that speak to the power and
eternal presence of the church, comes from the Greek word
meaning "kingdom of God." One is clearly meant to conjure
up images of the other in us—the church, the kingdom of
God; the kingdom of God, the church. I had an experience
some years ago, however, that ever since has made it very
hard for me to equate the two.

We were in the Basilica of the Immaculate Conception,
the National Shrine, in Washington, D.C. It was the opening

17

liturgy of the annual Bishops' Conference. A few of us, official observers to the meeting, were huddled alone together in one of the thick, dark pews halfway back in the center aisle of this great vacant void, waiting for the Mass to begin, like sparrows in a charred open field. The shrine, except for us, was completely empty. Suddenly, the organ roared and filled the yawning emptiness of the place like thunder on a dry summer day.

Then, heavy on their feet, they came marching down the aisle: two hundred and fifty of them in white cassocks and colored stoles, the light of the clerestory windows shining off their miters. I had never seen so much pomp for so little circumstance. I had never felt smaller and less part of the church. I had never felt more like a kind of uninvited guest in my own house, a pathetic kind of party crasher at the gate of heaven. Clearly, to be laity was to be a useless and unnoted appendage to the real thing. But then, all of a sudden, when the procession had finally ended and all the concelebrants were in place together far in front of us, one lone bishop in black pants and a white, open, short-sleeved shirt—tall, thin, stately, quiet—slipped into the pew beside us, bowed his head just a bit and smiled. Lo and behold, a bishop. The real thing.

At the end of the liturgy, the woman religious beside me handed me a folded Mass program. On the blank back of it she had meticulously drawn two hundred fifty cross-topped miters. Under the cartoon she had written, "We had a mitered good time." I laughed a little, but not really.

In the stark separation between the clerical church and its observers, I had seen the situation clearly: There is a difference between religion and spirituality. There is a link between them, of course, but one is not meant to be the other.

Religion is about what we believe and why we believe it. It is about the tradition, the institution, the system. Constructed over centuries—more than five thousand years ago for Hinduism, the first formal religion—religion draws for the world a portrait of creation and relationships. It gives us creeds and dogmas and definitions of God. It gathers us in worship and reminds us of a world to come.

Spirituality is about the hunger in the human heart. It seeks not only a way to exist, but a reason to exist that is beyond the biological or the institutional or even the traditional. It lifts religion up from the level of the theoretical or the mechanical to the personal. It seeks to make real the things of the spirit. It transcends rules and rituals to a concentration on meaning. It pursues in depth the mystical dimensions of life that religion purports to promote.

When we develop a spiritual life that is beyond some kind of simple, unthinking attachment to an inherited canon of behaviors, the soul goes beyond adherence to a system to the growth of the soul. Spirituality seeks to transcend the functionaries of religion to achieve an intimacy of its own with the mystery of the universe. Spirituality takes religion into its own hands.

Religion gives us commandments. The rules, layer upon layer of them over the centuries, purport to guide the way we live so that we can become what we seek. Religion prescribes a way through life in rites and customs that are meant to maintain an eternal order that the soul does not yet understand. The rules are meant, apparently, to lead to the Divine Reality that requires them. It is the rule keeping, the system leads us to understand, that defines both the boundaries and the quality of our spirituality.

Every day of my life I become less and less sure of that.

"Spirituality is expressed in everything we do," Anne E. Carr wrote in the journal. And I wrote back,

> I believe that our lives are our spirituality but I am not sure that behavior is its best test, its certain indicator. I do a great many things that "look" good: I suppress anger, I give partial responses to serious questions, I hold myself to my own breast and live life within life within life that no one else knows about. But at the same time, I long desperately to bring all of them into focus, into line, into the One, where the heart is soft toward everything and everyone in this world. So which approach is real spirituality?

Religion ends, in other words, where spirituality begins.

Religions are systems designed to lead humans to the divine. Religious professionals of every ilk devote themselves to maintaining the traditions that in their minds do that best. They all become bearers of a way. Some ways are very detailed, others remain more generic, but all of them are prescriptive and defining.

These witnesses to the way provide a kind of landmark by which to chart our own movements toward the light. We can see the cross, or the star, or the lotus, or the half-moon before us, calling us on. Or, we sense that it is behind us, calling us back. Or, we come to feel that it is beside us, giving us strength as we go. In the measurement of the distance between where the tradition would have me be and where I am now, I know the depth of the water in which my soul is wading. Sometimes I know I'm floating in a sea of eternal possibility. At other times, I know I'm in a desert that cannot possibly quench the thirsts of the soul.

Religion is meant to be light, sign, watermark, path. Religion becomes a map to a place no one has ever been. But the going on is up to me. And the way I go on is my spirituality.

For some, spirituality lies in the awareness of God in nature. For some, the cosmic God emerges through a life of service. For others, spirituality involves the development of meditative states that open the door to the nothingness that our complex and complicated lives otherwise obstruct. But for everyone, spirituality is not what we do to satisfy the requirements of a religion; it is the way we come into contact with the Holy. However we do it, whatever form or shape it takes—the mantra of devotions, the rhythms of nature, the faces of the other, the mysterious nothingness of deep meditation—spirituality makes real what religion talks about.

Religion is meant to bring us to spirituality. But spirituality brings people to religion, as well. Some people who haven't gone to church for years are still very tied to it in psychological ways and never go beyond it. Others go to church or services every week and know that though their bodies are one place, their souls are another. Many go to church, but go other places, too, in order to satisfy the spiritual needs in them that their churches do not. In every audience I meet, someone comes up to tell me that they "were a Catholic once." And I know as I hear the words, that down deep, more than likely, in some ways, they still are, despite themselves. What forms us lives in us forever. The important thing is that it not be allowed to stunt our growth.

Ironically, we often forget the very attitude most essential to the spiritual search: God is greater than religion. God is the spirit within us that calls us to the deep, conscious living of a spiritual life. God is the question that drives us beyond facile answers. God is the invisible vision that drives us to the immersion of the self in God.

Religion is the mooring of the soul. Spirituality is its lodestone. Religion is, at best, external. Spirituality is the internal distillation of this externalized witness to the divine.

Spirituality is what galvanizes us to do more than go through the motions. It spurs us to fill up the lack we feel within us. It is the desire for wholeness that evades us. It is the burning need to find the more.

The very purpose of religion is to enable us to step off into the uncharted emptiness that is the spiritual life, freely but not untethered. We have under our feet the promise of the tradition that formed us and the disciplines that shaped our souls. We can then wander through the pantheon of spiritual traditions freely, going deeper and deeper into every question from every direction. In the end, then, we become more, not less, of what we ourselves know to be our own religious identity.

It isn't so much that people leave religion, I think, as it is that, like Olympic runners on a mission, they come to a moment in life when they go on beyond the system to the very source of the light. It is the plight of the mystic to enter the universe of God alone where no charts or maps or signs exist to guide us and assure us of the way. It is a serious and disturbing moment, one after which we are never quite the same.

Commitment to the spiritual life makes demands on us, yes, but if we go deeper than the system to the God it promises, commitment frees us as well. Being spiritual means that we become more than pursuers and purveyors of a system. It requires a total change of heart, a total concentration of mind. "The journey of ever-greater spiritual awareness is not to be undertaken lightly," Margaret Guenther wrote. And I wrote in reply,

> I am a child of two generations whose watermark is Vatican II. Before Vatican II, the spiritual journey was an exercise in fear and guilt. After Vatican II, the spiritual journey became

a walk toward wholeness in the presence of a beckoning God. I find myself vacillating between those two even to this day. Sometimes the journey is full of joy, sometimes full of despair that it will ever come to fulfillment. But it is never done lightly.

Religion gives us the structures that weld the habits and disciplines of the soul into one integrated whole. Those same structures can also, however, smother the very spirit they intend to shape. We can get caught in the structures and the forms that are the basilica of religion. We can be overcome, even repulsed, by the power of God incarnated in ecclesiastical pomp. We can make the mistake of thinking that God and religion are synonyms and make religion God. We can, as the general semanticists teach us, mistake the way for the thing and the thing for the way.

"Glory in God's holy name; let the hearts of those who seek God rejoice," Psalm 105 reminds us. In the light of that verse, after years of struggling between both religion and spirituality, I wrote to myself,

> The danger in this psalm is that what is really being said here might well be missed entirely. At first glance, it seems to be talking about praise: "Glory in God's holy name." But what is embedded in the verse is an explanation of exactly who it is who has the right to "glory." It is not the perfect one. It is the one who seeks. It is the seeking that counts.
>
> It's so easy to forget that simple truth in a capitalistic society that teaches us to win, get, have, amass, and defines the best of us as the one who has the most of all those things. But in the God-life, the seeking is itself the end. We never "get" God but we always "have" God. We never "find" God but we forever dwell in God. So, if I'm seeking God, I have already come to God. And that is the height of spirituality.

Spirituality is a commitment to immersion in God, to the seeking that has no end. It is a consciousness of engrossment in God that defies convention, that lives beyond convention, that eclipses convention. Religion, the finger pointing at the moon, is not the moon. Simply keeping the rules, accepting the conventions, and loving the pomp that comes with religion will not get us there. For that we need a spirituality of search.

THE INWARD LIFE:
A DISCOVERY OF
THE OBVIOUS

When we live most deeply in our own hearts, we also live in the very heart of God.

—Jean M. Blomquist

The deepest part of me is the best part of me. It is the most honest, the most prayerful, the most compassionate. Clearly it is the closest to God. And it is inside myself that I hear God most acutely, as well. There the voice of God is not blocked by canons and customs and statements of ecclesiastical power.

—Joan Chittister, Journal, July 31

BY THE TIME I MET HER, SHE HAD THE AURA OF THE ancient. She was also brisk and strong and very, very free-spirited. At first sight you would have called her eccentric, but as I got to know her better—if anyone ever really knew Sister Hildegund—I called her holy.

She was one of our old German nuns, too deaf to talk to us, but not too deaf to hear the kitchen cat meow for food. She bustled around the monastery, stoop-shouldered and snuffling, slamming cupboard doors, banging pots and pans, and talking to herself. She was the community coif maker. She was seventy years old, and I was her seventeen-year-old novice apprentice.

All day Saturday, every Saturday, I sat at one pleating machine in her bedroom, while she sat at another. Galvanized metal washtubs full of linen sat between us. All day long, she thumped cloth-covered building bricks down on wet linen headgear to keep the pleats in place for drying while she talked to God. Out loud. One set of noises drowning out the other. I became fascinated by the patter, intrigued by the conversations. Sometimes Hildegund sang to God. Sometimes she scolded God.

Upstairs, in religion class, they were talking to us about "union with God" and "ascetical theology" and "contemplation." Downstairs, I decided, Hildegund had it. I was also pretty sure that she didn't understand a word the teachers were teaching about it. And I'm dead sure she didn't care.

One thing, however, was almost embarrassingly clear: Hildegund and God were a pair. But was I seeing insanity or sanctity? Was this theology or piety? And was there any difference between the two? Was God really this close to us, and if so, how do we all achieve that?

I haven't stopped wondering about those things yet. Nor, it seems, have any of the spiritual scholars. To this day we go on reading desert spirituality for its sense of Godness, however bizarre some of its demonstrations of that may seem to us now. We study Celtic spirituality for its links to nature and the struggle between pantheism and panentheism. We follow Orthodox spirituality for its use of image and its emphasis on the transcendence of the spiritual life and wonder aloud at the distinction between images and idols. We look to Western spirituality for its awareness of the incarnational and worry about the loss of a sense of mystery there. In every realm of every spiritual tradition, humanity searches for the secret to the Way.

The perennial question, centuries old and ever new, harries us: What is the spiritual life? How do we develop it? Is it real? Is it possible? Is it even desirable? Isn't earth about earth and heaven time enough for heaven? The questions plague us in the deepest parts of ourselves, to the blackest recesses of our souls. "We live most of our life," Wendy Miller wrote, "oblivious to our true identity as persons created and provided for by God." The starkness of the statement catapults us into another dimension of religion entirely. To know our true identity—to really know down deep where we came from, to whom we belong, out of whose life we live—is to know that the God who made us is with us still. God is the eternal memory, the inseparable presence, the unending energy that beats within us yet, inchoate but clear. I wrote back to myself,

> To live consciously aware of the presence of God in every moment is a great grace. I am still not sure if it is cultivated and then given—or given and then cultivated. I lean toward the latter position because it is my own experience. I never "merited" God. I simply grew in God. It is a very different thing. Church—sacraments—nourished the presence but, I am sure, did not create it. I would be in God with or without the Catholic Church.

The basic truth of the spiritual life, I am convinced, is that there are great mystics in every tradition. Mysticism is not a Western, Christian phenomenon. Mystics are people in whom the living God is a living reality, independent of denomination, irrespective of the brand of scriptures that underpin it. The Hindu Upanishads teach, "As rivers flow into the sea and in so doing lose name and form, even so the wise one freed from name and form, attains the Supreme Being, the Self-luminous, the Infinite." Rabia, the Muslim mystic, writes to God, "I have set up house for you in my heart."[1] The Jewish kabbalah teaches that we are all sparks of the divine. And the Tao te Ching, *The Book of the Way*, teaches, "The Tao is always present within you."[2] The God-life is no stranger to mystics anywhere; it is the very breath they breathe.

And, without doubt, it is in us, too. But the shape and cultivation of the God-life is a very personal thing. It touches each of us in the same way—and yet differently.

This sense of the presence of God is almost natural to many and a real struggle to some. But whatever our natural inclination for God, there are, nevertheless, some givens: We must be open to the God within us. We must be free of the shackles of the mind. We must be willing to forgo everything we have been told about God to this point. Count all of them wrong. Realize that all of them are inadequate, partial, well-meaning, but fallacious to a fault. We must not fear to go beyond proofs for the unprovable, or beyond belief to the unknown. Just because we do not know does not mean that we do not "know." As the Tao says, "The Way that can be told is not the eternal Way."[3]

Once we empty ourselves of our certainties, we open ourselves to the mystery. We expose ourselves to the God in whom "we live and move and have our being." We bare ourselves to the possibility that God is seeking us in places and people and things we thought were outside the pale of the God of our spiritual childhood. Then life changes color, changes tone, changes purpose. We begin to live more fully, not just in touch with earth, but with the eternal sound of the universe as well.

It's almost fifty years later and Sister Hildegund is long gone, but her time with me, I feel certain now, was well-spent. Now I'm the one who is talking to God.

Chapter Three

THE GOD WITHIN:
WHO SHALL I SAY SENT ME?

How does human language name God?

—Gail Ramshaw

*We name God poorly and we name God only partially always. As
a result, we never really "see" God. We only see the fragment of God
that we can bear to see: God's justice or God's mercy; God's anger
or God's tears. I had never seen the mother God, the nature God,
the waiting God, the teaching God until the last twenty-five years.
It has been a great loss.*

—Joan Chittister, Journal, July 2

I REMEMBER THE MOMENT VERY WELL. THE COMMUNITY
WAS at prayer. We were chanting the morning office together.
Those same psalms, I realized with a start, had been chanted
by some proportion of this community for almost one hundred fifty years. Generation after generation of Benedictine
women had been praying the same prayers. From one litur-
gical cycle to another, they had formed our minds and defined our theology. At the same time, it occurred to me, they
had been shaping our image of ourselves as well.

"Key of David" we had called God for over a century here and for centuries before that in Europe. We'd been singing God's praises as "Morning star, rock and refuge of sinners, gate of heaven, dove of peace, wind and fire and light," for century after century. They were awesome litanies, time-tested and true to the God who is everywhere. They soared in grandeur. They sang with power. They seduced the soul with the wonder of it all. God was every manner of image and metaphor and meaning the human mind could muster. And always, always, God was "God our Father."

At the same time, I began to realize—and here my heart stood still for a moment—we never, ever prayed to "God our Mother." God, the source of creation, God the Eternal Womb, was never—ever—recognized as a mothering God. We could call God "rock," "fire," "light," "wind," "bird," "door," "key," and "father," but never, ever "mother." It was a moment of soul-shaking revelation. Where were women in these images of God? And if they weren't there, what kind of God was this? And if they were there—or otherwise how could God really be the God of all being, all power, all life—then what kind of people were we that we refused to admit it? What were women in the economy of God? The answer was only too painful: We were invisible. I had given my life to a God who did not see me, did not include me, did not touch my nature with God's own.

"This is wrong," I said to a sister beside me. "We have to be patient," she said back with a smile. I couldn't help but wonder if two thousand years wasn't patience enough for her. I also had to wonder what it said about a woman's sense of self that she was willing to become invisible and be "patient" about it.

Finding a God big enough to be God was a spiritual task of no small proportions. I started over. If God is not God, or is at best only half a god, a male god, then where do we go? The Jewish Apocrypha teaches in reference to the picayune nature of the gods on Olympus, "If the Greek gods steal, by whom shall their believers swear."[4] I knew the feeling. When God cannot possibly be God, the soul loses hope that there is any God at all. And the heart goes dry.

But to confront the heresy of God the Father, I discovered quickly, is to be called a heretic. It is to come face-to-face with the possibility of exclusion, one way or another. We must accept the notion that God excluded femaleness from the Being that is God. Or, we must deal with the possibility that in reclaiming the fullness of what it means to be made "in the image of God," we may well be excluded from the community that taught us to believe that in the first place. To belong we must either diminish the very definition of God or demean the spiritual status of femaleness. A woman who is willing to do that mocks the God of creation. Any man who is willing to do that does not really want God at all. He simply wants himself writ large.

Those who claim to be keepers of the faith want a faith far smaller than a woman's soul can stand or the faith itself support. They claim to maintain a tradition, but they fail to recognize that the tradition they have in mind is more political than theological. It suits them, in other words.

Some people profit from such a system, no matter how deficient the thinking that supports it. They get power in it because they are closer to God, or they get "handmaidens" in it because women aren't. The system never changes because the people with the power to change it know that they would stand to lose power if they did. So, they say they can't change it because it has always been this way. And the circle goes round and round.

And that, of course, makes anyone who thinks otherwise a radical, an iconoclast, some sort of ecclesiastical anarchist. No matter that God's own name for God when Abraham asks in scripture, "Who shall I tell them sent me?" is not "I am your father," but "I am who am." Or to put not too fine a point on it: I am everything that is. I am pure being. The implications for the spiritual life, for the life of the Christian community, are astounding. By church standards, this is a very radical God.

As the issue of the nature and naming of God began to emerge more and more publicly, people leapt into the breach to save the faith for the Middle Ages. They argued for a now stone-dead science, which long ago assumed that since men were carriers of the seed of life—the only seed or semen they could see—God, who created everything, must then be male. It was a biology become defunct with an understanding of the nature of the ovum, of course, but theology had long since given up listening to science.

So the battle raged on about the Fatherhood of God, while women, in a new consciousness of their own discrete creation, became more and more alienated from the church of the fathers. Traditionalists saw it as an attack on religion itself. As the wag wrote, "A conservative is a person who believes that foolishness frozen in time is preferable to foolishness fresh off the vine." And foolishness we had had aplenty. What had always been taught, reactionaries reasoned, must therefore be true for the very reason that it had always been taught. But so had the notion of the flat Earth. In the light of contemporary science, the argument had ceased to persuade.

Men, "God's highest creature," theologians like Augustine taught and Thomas Aquinas later explicated, were closest to God. Males, in other words, are most like God. By virtue of their reason, men are "made in the image of God." Women, on the other hand, by virtue of their single function, generation, were deficient. Thomas Aquinas calls them "a necessary object who is needed to preserve the species and provide food and drink."[5] It had always been thus, they told us, and so must always remain.

Somewhere in the course of that kind of thought process, I began to realize that the God they were giving me to believe in was too small a God to possibly be worth a life. At least, not a woman's life.

What's more, I found that this God did not lead to God at all. If the God we say we worship, the God of all being, lacks the feminine—rejects the feminine—then this God is not God. This God is lacking in being. And the being of woman lacks something of God.

It is not easy to find the way back to the essence again once an image is cast in stone. This image of the superior male and a male God had been taught in male institution after male institution for centuries. By this time, it had done an untold amount of damage to the image of woman. Worse than that, it had completely blinded us to God.

But the search for God is the spiritual quest, the eternal journey, the breadth and depth and height of the universe. To find God means to be obliged to search beyond the images of limitation, to the essence, to the mystery, to the spirit. "God," Juanita Helphrey wrote, "is a cloud forming, an eagle soaring, a voice from the wilderness echoing through your ear." And so I considered my own understandings carefully and wrote,

God is. God is love. God made woman, too, in God's own image. . . . Those three sentences have become enough for

35

me. They have become my life. They sustain me; they caution me; and they drive me on. There is not much time left
now and these are the ideas that go with me into "The Val-
ley of Death." Not the doctrines, not the dogmas; not the
so-called "definitive" statements about the otherness of
woman—all of which are just one more example of male at-
tempts to capture the power of God for themselves.

This time the God I sought was big enough to be the
God of Being. No other spiritual idea has had as major an
effect on my life, on my sense of self and of my sense of the
real meaning of God as the God, who as well as being Father is also "God my Mother."

Chapter Four

THE PRESENCE OF GOD:
THE TRUTH THAT SETS US FREE

Silence is the best response to mystery.

—Kathleen Norris

We can't bear mystery, we can't abide the beneficence of the un-known. We "define" the nature of God, the substance of the Holy Spirit, the persons of Jesus. We dogmatize the unknown and we ex-communicate people who dare to wonder. I find it very hard any-more to abide the dogmatizers though I sometimes admire the sincerity of their "faith." Or is "faith" simply another term for the compulsion to know, and the willingness not to think.

—Joan Chittister, Journal, September 30

T HE SPIRITUAL LIFE AS I GREW UP IN IT WAS A TANGLE of double messages: "Sin separates us from God," they told us on one day. "God is everywhere," they told us the next. We were to strive to become holy, they told us, as if the en-terprise had something to do with doing holy things—meaning, apparently, whatever things they told us were holy. And, the message was clear, holiness depended entirely on us. If we were faithful—meaning if we kept the rules—God would reward us with heaven. If not, nothing could save us. At the same time, they also told us that "Faith was a gift," and no one could merit it.

The spiritual life, I learned very young, loomed outside of us, fraught with anxiety. You could spend your whole life being "good"—and suddenly, one day, slip. Then, before you knew it, you would find yourself in the bowels of hell, doomed for all eternity. All the rest of it, all the efforts and the sacrifices and the prayers, had been for nothing.

It worried me in second grade. It worried me for years. It created in one generation after another the neurotic mentality of confession manuals. There were multiple varieties of every sin. Some of the sins were minor, some major. This many ounces of food, this many minutes at the dinner table, constituted the Lenten fast, the laws said. One ounce more, one more hour, and the jig was up. Whatever forgiveness or sense of the healing presence of God confession brought, we knew, would be, at best, temporary. Having slipped in the past, we would certainly slip again.

This God was a devilish God, indeed. Commanding you to be holy, this God lay in wait for you to sin. The memory of Jonathan Edwards's Puritan sermon, "Sinner in the Hands of An Angry God," on the horrors of eternal damnation colored the whole spiritual life. God the Judge ruled the world, and no one was found innocent.

It's fashionable to laugh at those memories now. It's common to retell the horror stories as a kind of religious catharsis. But down deep, where we measure the relationship between God and self, people still remember the gritty, dirty feel of the hidden self and wince. The specter of it lived on in every family.

Uncle Lou, for instance, had married a Protestant girl. So, he simply stopped going to church. Why go? There was no use. He had no intention of leaving his wife and children. She had no intention of getting her marriage "fixed" in a church that insulted her conscience and disparaged her own religion. He knew he was lost forever, so why try.

In the end, Uncle Lou and Aunt Bert lived together for almost fifty years, faithful to one another, loving, and the glue of our whole extended clan. The nieces and nephews loved him. The brothers and sisters depended on his good heart and kind justice. It was hard to consider him damned.

The contradictions in all these situations bothered me in a kind of subconscious/conscious way. But they never bothered me enough for me to have the courage to wonder aloud how it was that public sinners could be beloved and my family not. Solomon with all his wives and David with all his ruthlessness were close enough to God to be elect, while my mother—who taught me how to pray, sent me to a Catholic school in the face of great opposition, and never cheated a person in her life, but who did not go to Mass on Sundays—was not. It took years to confront the inconsistencies in those things. It took half a lifetime to get to the point where fear no longer held my soul in thrall to the God of the system, but captive instead to the God of the woman taken in adultery.

It was years later in the monastery that things began to clear up for me. There, in a Rule of Life that was almost fifteen hundred years old, the message was clear. "The first degree of humility," this ancient document taught, "is to keep the 'fear'—the awe, the awareness—of God ever before our eyes." We were, the Rule insisted, to concentrate on God, not on sin. We were about awe, about awareness, not terror.

The message made plain what had been, at most, doubtful for years. God did not stay at a distance from us to toy with us. God was not close when we were perfect and far away when we were not. God was ours for the asking. God was with us. Here. Now. That was it. No questions asked.

What we needed to cultivate, then, was simply the *Memoria Dei*, the memory of God. We didn't earn God. We didn't ever deserve God. We couldn't possibly deserve God. We simply had God. God was of the essence of our lives. We only had to be conscious of God and grow into the life force that already lived in us.

How could we possibly forget such an obvious truth when the Scriptures speak so clearly about the God who went before the Israelites in the cloud by day and the fire by night and of the Jesus who became flesh and walked among us? "We look for God in the ordinary events of daily lives," Nancy Berneking and Pamela Carter Joern wrote in the journal, "and listen for God in lived experiences." Once I understood the simplicity of the situation I could write back with confidence,

> God, scripture assures us, is not in the whirlwind. God is not in a plethora of anything—words, places, rituals, ecclesiastical games, or people. God is simply right where we are. Which, of course, is why God is so hard to find. We are always looking elsewhere. "There," says the church. "There," says the society. But God is here—right here—all the while.

The clear, conscious recognition that God is with us—whoever we are, whatever we are, wherever we are—makes God, God. It is not our virtue that captures God, like salt on the tail of a bird. It is simply of the nature of God to be in and with creation. In and with all of us. All the time. The simple truth, the obvious truth of it, gives the lie to merit theology. We don't have to merit God, monastic theology teaches. We have God. It is not God we're missing. It is the awareness of God in the commonness of life that we fail to cultivate.

"Mindfulness teaches us to be fully aware of each experience, letting nothing remain unnoticed, taking nothing for granted," Holly Whitcomb's journal entry read. And after years of monastic life, I could write back,

> Mindfulness is the arch monastic virtue. Maybe that's why monastics choose small cells, unfrequented places, simple surroundings. After all, it can take a lifetime to really see flowers, feel wood, learn the sky, walk a path and hear what all these things are saying to us about life, about our own growth, about the spirit in the clay of us. But once mindfulness comes, life changes entirely.

Suddenly, a sense of the eternal presence of God consumed me. The monastic emphasis on awareness became the counterpoint to my whole notion of the spiritual life. Consciousness of the God of the universe, who is in us, as well as around us, changed my entire perspective of both who God is and who I am.

Then, I understood. Life is not about getting God. Life is about growing in God.

The implications of that simple awareness, for me, were life-changing: I began to see that God is my reality. "God called me from the womb," Isaiah says, "and from the body of my mother. God named my name." And I noted in my journal,

> God is my womb: In God "I live and move and have my being." . . . There is, I think, a "call" deep in the human heart, a magnet that takes us first to our true selves and from there into a consciousness of the God who is the call. I have known the call and still know the call as a vivid, daily

vibration in my body. Early in life I searched for God but knew nothing but the search. In 1960, God found me and has never left—unfaithful, disinterested, distracted as I have been and am.

I began to see that the spiritual life is much simpler than I had been led to believe.

"Spiritual journal writing can . . . be a way of discovering what we truly believe," Elaine Ward wrote. And knowing something more now than that God was distant and remote and watching and counting, I could finally write back,

> I find that my beliefs grow simpler, more focused every day: God is, Jesus goes before us, life is One. Where we are—the culture we're in, the faith we hold—is not the only manifestation of God in the world or even, perhaps, its best one. Everything beyond the simple awareness of God is gift, fortuitous, and maybe. In *In Search of Belief* I worked hard to believe. But "belief," in the canonical or theological sense of the word, is not necessary. It is presence that matters—and I have had the presence since I was twenty-four years old.

It is the presence of God that is for our taking. And once we take it, nothing else counts for much. Maybe that's what the evangelist John meant when he said, "You shall know the truth—and the truth shall set you free." Free from what? Free from fear, of course.

Chapter Five

PRAYER:
EVERY TIME I DO GET TIME

It is through prayer . . . that one will be given the most powerful light to see God and self.

—Angela of Foligno

"To see God" is to care very little about anything lesser. But in prayer I see my own littleness most clearly. I know how cowardly I really am. My voice is but one drop of water in an ocean of op‑ pression. It will not change the ocean. But it may put it in need of explaining the injustice it can no longer hide, perhaps. I cannot not speak what my heart knows to be true.

—Joan Chittister, Journal, March 5

THE HALLMARK OF A BENEDICTINE COMMUNITY LIES IN its prayer life. The community gathers for choral prayer at least three times a day—morning praise, noon praise, and vespers. In Benedictine communities that devote themselves to the recitation of the more ancient Liturgy of the Hours, the times for communal prayer are even more often than that. To beginners in the life, the schedule can be a shock.

When we were in the novitiate, the old sisters delighted in telling us the story of the young postulant who came to the monastery full of zest for the life—and then, six months later, simply got up and left. "I like it here a lot," the young woman is declared to have said, "but there's never a minute's rest. And every time I do get time, the bell rings." Then the old sisters would bubble over with the kind of laughter that is private and personal. They knew why the story was funny. We did not.

It took a while before I caught on to the joke. The funny part was that the postulant had the ideas confused. She didn't get it. She couldn't understand why it was that every time the chores of the day were finished, just when she thought she wouldn't have anything to do for a while, the bell rang to call the community to another period of prayer. Prayer for her was work, an intrusion into her private time. But for those whose life is centered in prayer, prayer is time for resting in God. It is the "work" of the soul in contact with the God of the heart.

Prayer is what links the religious and the spiritual, the inner and the outer dimensions of life. Every spiritual tradition on earth forms a person in some kind of regular practice designed to focus the mind and the spirit. Regular prayer reminds us that life is punctuated by God, awash in God, encircled by God. To interrupt the day with prayer—with any centering activity that draws us beyond the present to the consciousness of eternal truth—is to remind ourselves of the timelessness of eternity. Prayer and regular spiritual practices serve as a link between this life and the next. They remind us of what we are doing and why we're doing it and where our lives are going. They give us the strength of heart to sustain us on the way. When life goes dry, only the memory of God makes life bearable again. Then we remember that whatever is has purpose.

It took years of repetition, years of chant strung high as a wire, years of recitation droned into space for me to realize that like water on a rock, the words were melting into my soul, etching furrows in my mind, turning me into themselves, disappearing into the whispers of my heart. Prayer, the regular discipline of resting in God, had become a way of life.

But prayer has issues of its own. The journal raised one of them quite clearly. "The more you pray," Angela of Foligno wrote, "the more you will be enlightened." But I knew better:

> The statement, as it stands, is both true and false. When we turn God into a vending machine, when we pray to "get" things rather than to get God—there is no "enlightenment" in that. When prayer is a journey into the mind and heart of God, into the nature of life, into the shaping of a holy heart, then it is necessarily enlightening. We come to understand ourselves: our fears, our darkness, our struggles, our resistance. Then we are faced with choice. That is enlightenment.

Prayer does not simply reveal us to God and God to us, I had come to know after years of apparently useless repetition. It reveals us to ourselves at the same time. If I listened to myself when I prayed, I could feel my many masks drop away. I was not the perfect nun; I was the angry psalmist. I was the needy one in the petitions. I was the one to whom the hard words of the gospel were being spoken. I was the one adrift in a sea of darkness and uncertainty even after all these years of light.

The round of daily prayer became the way I was brought to encounter myself so that the work of coming to God could really begin.

It is inside myself, in the cavern that is the soul, that prayer really happens. It is not a string of absentminded mutterings. It is confrontation with the emptiness of me. Then the God who reveals that void can come in to fill it. Without prayer, without conscious attention to the incompleteness in me, God cannot come in. Without that, I have no need of God. A magician maybe, but not God. There is a silent dimension to even choral prayer because then God is doing the communicating. "Praying brings us into the presence of God who loves us," the journal entry read. And now I could write back,

> But after a while, it seems to me, no words are necessary. We come to live in the presence of God at all times. Words are simply what tie us to the distractions between here and full immersion into the Energy which is God. If we pray long enough, we cease to pray; we become a prayer.

"I don't pray," people say to me. And I say back, "Neither do I. I just breathe God in and hope somehow to learn how to breathe God out, as well."

The purpose of prayer is simply to transform us to the mind of God. We do not go to prayer to coax God the Cornucopia to make our lives a Disneyland of possibilities. We don't go to prayer to get points off our sins. We don't go to suffer for our sins. We go to prayer to be transfigured ourselves, to come to see the world as God sees the world, to practice the presence of God, to put on a heart of justice, of love, and of compassion for others. We go to become new of soul.

The irony of prayer is that the very act of prayer itself can delude us into thinking that we're spiritual people. If prayer is recitation for the sake of ritual, then it is possible to pray and pray and never change at all.

46

If prayer is not a spiritual vending machine, it is also not meant to be an escape from life. Every spiritual faddist wants it to be so, of course. But if prayer becomes the way we give ourselves permission to escape life around us, it is not prayer. It is some kind of self-induced hypnotism, at best. Real prayer plunges us into life, red and raw. It gives us new eyes. It shapes a new heart within us. It leaves us breathless in the presence of the living God. It makes demands on us—to feed the hungry and clothe the naked, give drink to the thirsty and take care of the sick. It requires that we become the hands of the God we say we have found.

A community takes time out for prayer every day of life in order to remember why they work as hard as they do taught me long ago to beware the kind of "rest" that prays in order to keep the world out. "Our prayerful listening to God softens the hard and busy paths that still crisscross our heart," Wendy Miller wrote. And I answered her,

> I like Miller's concept—but I also question it. In my life, at least, the "hard and busy paths" are often the very voice of God I most need. "Prayerful listening" can be a temptation to ignore these other voices in order to escape into the holy magic of "prayerfulness." On the other hand, without prayer, I doubt that I would ever have heard those voices at all. The psalms keep me real.

Our greatest mystics were our most real people, our hardest workers, our most feeling exemplars of what it was to live life fully. Catherine of Siena, Teresa of Avila, Charles de Foucauld, Ignatius of Loyola, Elizabeth Seton, Martin of Tours, Dietrich Bonhoeffer, Dorothy Day, Mahatma Gandhi, and Martin Luther King Jr. lived in God and wept with the people around them.

Maybe we are forgetting to center ourselves in the consciousness of the God who is conscious of all of us. Maybe that's why the world today is in the throes of such brutal violence, such inhuman poverty, such unconscionable discrimination, such self-righteous fundamentalism. Maybe we are forgetting to pray, not for what we want, but for the sight, the enlightenment, that God wants to give us.

And if I pray, will I be able to change those things? I don't really know. All I know is that the enlightenment that comes with real prayer requires that I attend to them, not ignore them.

Chapter Six

THE CALL OF GOD:
AN ECHO IN THE HEART

Walk in the light and carry that light to chase away the shadows in which so many dwell.

—Lavon Bayler

There is such a thing as "the light." I have known it for years: It is the steady, steady awareness that what is going on in life is "right" for you—no matter how bad it may feel at the time. I have known darkness aplenty, yes, but the light that came out of it is brighter than ever. As a result, I must spend my own life trying to bring it.

—Joan Chittister, Journal, January 6

LIFE IS A SERIES OF POSSIBILITIES, ONE LARGE GRID OF entrances and exits, highways and byways, directions and decisions that cross and conflict with one another, all of them promising fulfillment. Each of them lies just one more tantalizing step beyond reach of what we think will surely fulfill us, certainly make us completely happy, finally give us what we want. And so we grasp at every infatuation restlessly. We run riot up and down the roads of life always looking for new directions, for sure gain, for certain success.

We try one. And then another. And then another. Until eventually we discover that in all our going we have gotten to nowhere that we recognize as home. The search is relentless; the finding is always incomplete.

What is to be made of such a thing? Do we all live life wrongly, or is life only lived on the run, an endless, but fruit-less, scurrying from one dead end to another? Or, perhaps, is the search itself the essence of life?

The fact is that each of life's roads goes somewhere dif-ferent. And all of them sparkle and beguile. All of them run the risk of leading us away from the center of the self. We set out to swallow the universe and wind up too often starved for life.

Some of the roads go to money. Some of them go to the heaping up of "grain in barns," as the Scripture de-scribes accumulation for its own sake. Some of them go to excitement and variety and stimulation. Some of them go to independence or security. Some of them go to status. But where they go is almost never the point. Any road is a good road as long as it takes us where, at the deepest center of the self, we know that we should be. It's the road that takes us to a sense of the fulfillment that we really seek. It's the road on which, having reached the end, we say to ourselves, "Yes, finally."

The most haunting question in life is, Which one of those roads really leads to the self? Which one of them brings us home to the part of us that nothing else satisfies? Which one of them, without it, leaves us living shells of the person we know ourselves to be? Which one of them takes us beyond fear of loss and fear of others to a sense of spir-itual invincibility, to the awareness that nothing and no one can deter us from what we are meant to do, that nothing and no one can take anything away from us that can possibly touch the center of the self? It's an important spiritual question, because the road that goes to the self is the one that goes to God.

The journal was clear. "For the gifts and call of God are irrevocable," Paul writes in the Letter to the Romans. And I got the message. I wrote,

> I like this. It's straight: We have a purpose in life and we are given within us whatever it takes to do it. All we need is the will and the courage to be what we are supposed to be. Then, everything else in life gets focused on it, gets caught up in it, gets filtered through it, gets measured by our fidelity to that call.

The spirituality of the nineteenth and early twentieth century, spawned in a world of coal mines and assembly lines, taught an offer-it-up philosophy of survival. Gone were the farmers and the artisans who gave themselves to their work and became new themselves because of it. Now, work became what a person did to make a living, rather than to make a life.

But everybody lives to do something that only they can do. Everyone of us is called, by virtue of what we love and what we do well, to give something to the world that will bear the stamp of our presence here. We are all called to add something to the creation of the universe.

The question is, How? And the answer must surely be by using what there is in us that we do best.

My journal confronted me with words that I had been hearing for years from the First Letter of Peter. "You have been born anew, not of perishable seed but of the imperishable, through the living and abiding word of God." The words brought me up short. I heard a clanging sound within me.

> I don't know if I have been "born anew" or not but I do know that something new is trying to be born in me. The question is whether or not it may not be a bastard child—unwanted, illegitimate, disruptive. Whatever it is, it lurks inside fighting for breath. If I repress it, I may never be real, never be true, never be a writer in the truest sense of the word. But if I let it grow, I may be none of those things anyway. And yet, how else do we test the Spirit?

I know too many people who have not tested the spirit within them and died inside, even while they went on living.

A friend of mine went from accounting job to accounting job, grinding out one set of numbers after another and wishing all his life that he had gone into woodworking. He went into accounting to have a steady job and resented its sameness, its steadiness, all his life.

A student of mine, a brilliant debater, an excellent history student, majored in math in college. His father insisted that there were "better opportunities in math," which, translated, meant that there was more money to be made in math than in the liberal arts. In the end he failed the higher math courses and had to change majors. It was an experience that ate away at his self-confidence all the rest of his life.

I myself postponed writing for years in order to concentrate on teaching and administration, both of them good for me, but neither of them enough to open up the other whole part of me.

The point is that we are never at home with ourselves until we have come to be what we know ourselves to be inside. And what we are inside, we are born with and meant to unleash. But all too often—for social approval or fear of risk

or neurotic self-doubt or quick gain—we have learned to resist the call of God to full development with might and
main. We stay where we are because we prefer the security of
the present to the possibility of the future. My journal
wrested the truth out of me. Mary Borhek wrote, "One of
the marvelous facts of life is that every ending carries within
itself the potential for a new beginning." I wrote in return,

> I have had to learn this truth the hard way—and may not
> really have learned it at all. Whatever the public perception,
> I find it very difficult to give up the past. My pattern is to
> resist it kicking and screaming. But then, once the step is
> taken, never to look back. I simply am where I am—rooted
> until I go through the next forcible replanting—and then I
> root again. So far every planting has been a better one.
> When will I ever learn that?

We are each called to something. Discovering where it is that
God will break out in us in full becomes the major task of life.

"Call" sinks its talons into our hearts. The awareness
that we are yet meant to do more than we are signals where
God lies in wait for us to become what we are meant to be.
Then the spiritual life, the awareness of a driving energy
within that is greater than ourselves, greater than anything
around us, begins to happen. We give ourselves over to what
is even greater than the self, the idol to which we had previ-
ously devoted our lives.

We cease to live for the self alone. We walk with God
now. We begin to make cosmic plans; we begin to make
things happen that co-create the world, rather than simply
soothe the ego. We begin to rebuild life in the model of the
gospel. Spirituality requires that we release the spirit in ourselves. Most of all, it implies that we must follow the road
to the innards of our souls. "No one knows what lies

ahead," Jan Richardson's journal entry said, "when we say yes to God." After having lived through years of good works, but false starts, I wrote back,

> I can only trust that what lies ahead will be fuller, freer, than the present. I hope for a life that is my own, that has no false chains to bind me, that allows me to move like a butterfly on the wind and to stand, when necessary, like a lioness in high grass. I want a life that is directed by the call within myself—not by an institution, not even by what looks like the care and concern of others.

When we find at the core of our being what God has planted in us for our tilling and reaping, we will have found the God who is waiting for us. Then we will walk with God, singing all the way.

We make life an unending engagement with the systems to which we are beholden, however benign, however smothering they may be. We forget sometimes that God is the echo we hear in our hearts, totally independent of the systems, the certainties, to which we have fallen heir. To be what my father wants me to be, to do what my mother hopes I will do, to become what the institution says I should become, to succeed at the role in the way the world says the role must be played trap us outside of ourselves. We must, Thoreau reminds us, "Step to the music we hear, however measured or far away."

We must not, if we are to be spiritual people, fail to realize that life is meant to be nothing but a growing ground in God. If we fail to cultivate that part of us that is our truest self, how can the self come to full life in us? The spiritual life is the discovery of the self God meant us to be so that who we are can be God's gift to the rest of the world.

Chapter Seven

INSIGHT:
THE ALCHEMY OF EXPERIENCE

The people who sat in darkness have seen a great light.

—Matt 4:16

Maybe one of the great unknown—unrecognized—truths of life is that light always dawns, eventually; that there is no such thing as a perpetual darkness of soul. I know that in my own case the darkness only existed because I refused the light. I simply did not want the light. I had been in the cocoon of darkness for so long I thought that it was light.

Maybe life is simply a going from light to light, from darkness to darkness till the last Great Darkness signals the coming of the First Great Light. That would explain why we are in a constant state of "disillusionment." I have come to understand that it is not protesting what we do not like that counts. It is choosing what we do which, ultimately, changes things.

—Joan Chittister, Journal, January 24

TO APPRECIATE THE SUBTLETIES OF LIFE THESE DAYS, YOU have two choices. You can either read books of quotations by the great philosophers or you can buy posters and T-shirts.

I prefer the posters and the T-shirts. They tell me what people are really thinking right now on planet Earth, and, better yet, in my neighborhood. The folk wisdom walking down the street at me yesterday in cornrows and jeans was loud and clear. It was also correct. "Don't give up on me now," the shirt read. "God ain't finished with me yet." Maybe not, but I'm convinced that the God of life is working on it.

Life is an accumulation of becomings, all of them important, none of them complete.

I know a nun who left her religious order at the age of sixty-eight. It was Mother Teresa, and she left one congregation to begin another one.

I know a late-middle-aged woman who finally divorced her alcoholic husband when the eighth and last child left the home. She moved into an apartment alone, got herself a low-level clerical position, and ten years later, in her sixties, started a successful business of her own.

I know a young man who simply decided that life as we live it in a fast-paced, upwardly mobile United States was more "upwardly" oriented than his soul could bear. So, he worked in corporate America until he had enough investment capital to provide a decent middle-class income for his family and then quit to stay home with the children. Now, he consults on a part-time basis, but for the most part, he simply lives a slower, quieter life.

Everyone I know starts again sometime in life. I know that in my own case, I dealt with the tensions of my parents' mixed marriage, the struggles with polio, the tedium of teaching, and the interminable issues of administration—all of which taught me very important things about myself. In the end, I finally came to see that I needed all those things to become more than the person any single one of them could evoke in me. It is learning to accept the endings, to embrace the new beginnings, that makes all the difference.

I had been told that, of course, but it took years before the experience of all those losses, all those changes, became the message itself. The incident was a painful one: When the phone call came, I remember the shudder of intuition that went down my arms. Sister Theophane, they told me, one of the strongest, most intelligent, most formative people in my life, the woman because of whom I had finally recovered from polio, had collapsed at one of our small houses in the inner city. The ambulance was on its way, they said. From ten miles out of town, I made it to the house before the paramedics did. "I'm going now, Joan," she said when I dropped to my knees beside her. A nurse before she entered, a caretaker all her life, I had no doubt that she knew what she was saying.

"Sister," I pleaded like any young disciple in the throes of fear at the loss of a mentor, "Hang on. Please hang on. Don't go."

She was lying on the floor beside the bed with her eyes closed, her hands clutching her chest. "No, it's all right." she said. "It's over now."

I was desperate. "But, Sister," I could hear myself getting more insistent, "you can't go." I was fairly shouting now. "What about me!"

Her eyelids flickered for a second, she gave a long, tired breath, and she said very quietly, "History records, dear, that you will do quite well." Sister Theophane lingered for another forty days, but those were the last words she ever said. I have carried them in my heart ever since. They were a life lesson of immense proportion that simply went on growing and growing and growing in me.

The fact is that history records that we all really do quite well, however we do. Transitions complete us. We ripen. We learn. We hurt. We survive one thing after another. And we go on, whatever the odds against us. Then, in the end, we gain what we came to get—a kind of well-worn, hard-won wisdom. One way or another life batters us until we get the unavoidable. Sometimes we get it with glory; sometimes we get it in disgrace. Whatever the circumstances, the problem is that we all too seldom bother to stop and notice how much we have become in the process.

One day the entry in my journal was from Psalm 29. It read, "Ascribe to God the glory of God's name; worship God in holy array." I paused at the seeming remoteness of it for a moment. Then, I realized what it was that troubled me about the verse. I wrote,

> The God-idea is an overwhelming one. It means we are floating in a sea of security, living in the arms of eternity. So what is life all about? The worship of God? The praise of God? Well, maybe, but if it is, it sounds like a very narcissistic God to me. No, that can't be it. Life must be the womb of God. We are gestating. We are growing to the point where we are ready to melt into a life that is really the fullness of life. Wrapped in the holy array of a life well-lived, we find ourselves breathing the breath of God.

When Gus, a longtime friend, lay dying, we talked together about the movement down the birth canal as a difficult one which the fetus resists for as long as possible. And this despite the fact that life is better than gestation. Then we talked about the comparison of that to death, the birth canal to another kind of life. A better one. That process, I noted, we also resist. And the more I think about the comparison, the more I'm sure it's true. For that, indeed, God be praised.

We like to think that we achieve. We want to know that we have "arrived." But the self is a work in progress. It is the spiritual fashioning of a soul. And souls grow slowly. We spend life becoming ready to be human beings worthy of life. It is no small enterprise.

The journal carried a verse from Psalm 16, as well. It read, "You show me the path of life; in your presence there is fullness of joy." I realized when I thought about it that I had always prayed that verse as if it were the assurance that God makes directions clear. This time I understood it differently. I wrote,

> The problem with this psalm is that it promises a path but not a direction. It fails to point out that the path of life is too often a most circuitous one in a world that likes, in fact teaches, the virtue of straight lines. When I was growing up they asked you in eighth grade what you were going to be in life. And you were supposed to be able to tell them. Now people have three college majors before they graduate and four major jobs on their résumés before they're forty. Obviously, "The path of life" is much more than a simple career placement. It is an attitude of mind, an orientation of heart, a quality of soul, a sum of all learnings. Show me.

It is the learnings that life is all about, not the situations in which we learn them. Being vice president of the business or mayor of the village or dean of the college or *Time* magazine's "Person of the Year"—just when we think we have it all, in other words—may be exactly the moment when we learn humility. When we taste failure and survive it, when we find out what it is to lose everything, we finally stand to discover that, in the end, we really lost nothing of value at all.

Indeed, the learnings about the self may be simpler than we think. It may be little more than that final blinding recognition that the circumstances of life are much less important than what we learn about what it means to become fully human because of them. But if that is the case, then there is no such thing as a "wasted" life. There is no such thing as losing.

The spirituality of selfness is a keystone dimension of the spiritual life. It lies in negotiating the tensions between loving nothing but the self and loving everything but the self. It is a devil's bargain all the way, full of uncertainty, demanding of trust. It is a matter of keeping one eye on God at all times. "So often life offers up challenges to our minds, our spirits, even our very lives," Joan Brown Campbell wrote for the journal. I smiled when I read it. And I wrote back,

> No, it is not "'often" that life challenges us. It is always. I have lived the challenge for ten years now. Is it to finish what I began because I began it? Or is it to say, "That's over now. It has done all that it can do," and move on to explore the unknown? It is a genuine question. I know what I am here. But is that what I really am? All of it? And, at this moment in history, is this really what I should be?

Because life tests us, we must not fear to test life. Every decision must be revisited, every impulse evaluated. Then we will only be where we are because where we are is still right for us, still teaching us what we dearly need to know. Then, as long as we are learning, growing, becoming, "history will record that we have done quite well."

We do not do it alone, of course. We are companioned through life by those few who are strong when we are frail, wise when we are naive, certain when we are unsure. Underneath it all, holding us up as we change, are the people who love us. They make the present bearable and the future possible. However much we find ourselves in the throes of life, they stand by until we land again on solid ground, find ourselves again, get up in the morning ready to start over. Because of them, we stay steady on the path. They provide the unchanging foundations of love that enable us to risk change. But that is as much a spiritual truth as it is a personal one. "Love is the power," June Goudey wrote, "to act one another into well-being and God is love," the journal reminded me one day. After a season of changes and obstacles and weariness, I wrote back,

> The people who love us prod us—enable us—to grow. And God loves us. Maybe that is why I have been moved from one nest to another, all the way through life: God loves me and wants me to grow. I am trying, before I die, to learn to trust this continual going into the unknown. I better have a long, long life.

The Hebrew scriptures pray over and over again for "length of days." Long life we call a blessing. But, when long life brings hardship, as well—loneliness, loss, physical debilitation—why prolong it? And the answer surely must be because life is a spiritual journey that takes a lifetime to bring us to the fullness of the spiritual self, with all the spiritual insight life brings.

This coming to see things from the center of the soul may be life's greatest spiritual task. We don't "find" spirituality or "get" spirituality or "develop" spirituality. We are simply spiritual creatures who spend a great deal of our lives trying to avoid or deny or ignore the implications of that. But these meanderings of the self, the circuitous search for the life that is life, the reluctant surrender to new growth, finally shape a self for us to be. That is the spirituality of selfness. In the growing of that self is the alchemy of life that dissolves us into God. If only we will open our hearts to allow it.

Chapter Eight

SOLITUDE:
THE BALM OF THE SOUL

The unknown, hidden God of mystery is a final way of speaking of the God who is always more than human images . . . can suggest.

—Anne E. Carr

Interestingly enough, it may only be in mystery that we can see God at all. God is really more what we do not know than what we do know. "How can I be successful at contemplative prayer?" MD asked me yesterday. And all I could tell her was that the day she was "successful" she would know she had failed because God is always "more."

—Joan Chittister, Journal, August 11

I MET A HERMIT ONCE. SHE TOLD ME NOT TO BE ONE. I didn't expect it to turn out that way.

I had read a good deal about the solitary lifestyle. Since solitude and silence are part and parcel of Benedictine life, it only makes sense to assume that hermits would develop there. Well, maybe, but the fact is that hermits themselves are scarce on the ground in Benedictine communities, so I

looked forward to meeting this one. I had even written in my
own journal once,

> My greatest concern right now is what harm has been done
> to me by being where I am and doing what I do. I am a lot
> of things because I have been here. But I have given up a lot
> of things, too. I got a base, a context, a spirituality. I lost
> my freedom, my real solitude, maybe even a vocation of re-
> flection and study in the Camaldoli. I think of them more
> every day.

Now I would have a chance to talk about these things face-
to-face with someone who had already gone the road.

This particular hermit lived in a small two-room cot-
tage on the convent property of which she had once been
prioress. I walked out through the fields to the fenced-in cot-
tage, wondering what it had taken for her to make the break
with the community that such a step demanded. I wondered,
too, why more of us don't do it. I had written about it in my
journal more than once. I wrestled with Lavon Bayler's notion that we must "dwell consciously in God's presence in
the midst of all we do every day." And I wrote back,

> It is only this Presence—this and this alone—that has sus-
> tained me on this path since 1960. Once it came, I never
> lost it. It has never abandoned me. It is strong and clear.
> And, through everything, it has been enough for me. I have
> never felt the absence of God since. The question is, If I left
> here, would I leave that or would I know even more of it?
> That is a very determining question for which I have yet to
> know the answer.

The question of whether or not we are where God wants us
to be and whether leaving one kind of spiritual greenhouse

for another is tantamount to leaving God nibbles at the edges of the human mind.

The day was cool, and the breeze was fresh, but I could still feel in my bones the special kind of fatigue that comes from crossing one time zone after another. After all, I'd been carrying luggage from lecture site to lecture site for weeks. Jet lag was sucking the life out of me, slowing my responses, weighting down my legs. What's more, my soul was tired, too. I had been introduced to more people in a month than I ever expected to meet in a decade. I felt drenched with listening and dry from talking. I didn't really know how much longer I could go on doing this kind of thing.

So, sitting on the low straight-backed wooden chair in her sitting room, I took the plunge: I had thought a lot about being a hermit, too, I told her, rambling on about the toll that travel and talk take on a person after a while. Then I explained how, like her, I had lived through years of administration and all the wearying dailiness that kind of service brought with it. It occurred to me, I told her, that it was time for some drastic changes in my life. And, I added lamely, looking around the small sparse rooms, "I would love this."

The old hermit looked at me quietly. She did not actually smile, but her eyes softened a bit. "No," she said. "This is not for you. You are not a hermit. If you went to a hermitage, you would be a hermit like Thomas Merton. You would have friends coming over all the time."

The words, sparse as they were, tore away the gossamer fancies from across my mind. I was suddenly very alert. Solitude and a life of solitude, I understood in a flash of cold sober light, were two different animals. I wanted solitude— the kind of space that soothes the soul and eventually makes us useful to others again by enabling us to deal with the demons of the day. She, on the other hand, lived a life of

65

solitude—the kind of space that peels back the layers of the soul to the center of the self, a day at a time for years. It is a life of solitude that, after long whiles, exposes us to ourselves, one gremlin at a time, in full and total honesty. Then, nowhere to hide, nothing to distract us, we might eventually become open receptacles to the divine here and now and always.

The spiritual task of the serious life lies in distinguishing one from the other: the human need for solitude from the spiritual discipline of solitude. It is so easy to seduce ourselves into building a cocoon around ourselves and calling it contemplation. I knew the temptation of it only too well. The journal prompted me one day with a statement that unmasked the difference: "To have a flash of intuition or insight," Mary Borhek wrote, "is one thing. To begin to live by that new insight is quite another." And I responded,

> Just reading today's quotation freezes my breathing and turns my chest to stone. That is the problem: I have seen another life—aloneness—and cannot bring myself to live by that insight, to become what I've never been—an independent adult without an institution around my neck. Just a person without a schedule and free of a role long faded.

To go on going on is one thing; to live by insight is entirely another. I clearly wanted seclusion badly enough to confuse it with insight. I had peace, but I had yet to determine whether the desire for aloneness was really a spiritual call or simply the temptation to hide for a while.

The road to the real self is a steep one; it goes both up and down. It stretches us at one moment to the height of our most insidious hopes. Then, it dashes us at the next to the emptiest depth of our souls. Telling up from down takes no small amount of self-critical reflection. I have spent a lot of time going down the path to the demands of the self—and all in the name of going up the path to God. In this instance, I had clearly begun to confuse the need for physical rest with the thirst for mystery.

I had forgotten, if I ever knew until then, that withdrawal and contemplation were not the same things. The need to withdraw from the world around us can be either neurotic or spiritually therapeutic. It all depends on why we do it and what we want to get out of it. Withdrawal is both antidote and curative. But that's all it is. It is not a synonym for contemplation. Contemplation consists of an attitude of soul. When we steer by a sense of the encompassing presence of God, we live a contemplative life.

It wasn't contemplation I lacked. Contemplation drew me in like a great, engulfing wind. The journal was clear about that: "In the intensity, diversity and rapid pace of our daily lives," Elizabeth Francis Caldwell wrote there, "we must remember to reconnect the holy and sacred with the daily and the ordinary." And I wrote back without hesitation,

> It is precisely the notion of the separation of life into two spheres—one "daily" and one "sacred"—that bothers me most. It makes the spiritual life a schizophrenic experience. I have no time for it. Life has begun to merge for me into one long experience of God. Heaven has already begun—veiled and dim and dark, perhaps. But here. Definitely here.

No, it wasn't the sense of mystery I lacked. I lacked space and distance and a feeling of what it was to be human. The needs were clear, but I had missed them or denied them or failed to recognize that a person covets both. In another place in the journal, I discovered, I sounded the warning again. Wendy Natkong had written there, "The truth is, I had chosen to enjoy my own company for a while. Something I had never really done." And I wrote below her words,

> Being able to be alone—to be away and be alone—is the sweetest thing in life to me. It is the only time in life when I really feel like a free standing, fully developed, human, adult, being. I would love to spend the rest of my life like this. As it is, I will probably die an institutional robot, just like everyone else. But for me at least, it's wrong.

Contemplation had been a way of life for me. But the struggle for the solitude it takes to come to grips with the self, to repair the frayed parts of the soul, to rest in the arms of nothingness went on inside me, smoldering for attention. Then I met the hermit.

I learned something from her that I had never clearly understood about myself. Before the pressures of ministry began to build, I had known a love of both quiet and contemplation. Now, in the search for quiet, I had lost sight of the contemplative dimension of life. The spiritual danger zone had erupted inside of me. I was confusing one with the other. Contemplation was a spiritual need; quiet was a physical one. Unless I could distinguish one from the other and satisfy each, I stood to lose both. It was clearly a dangerous time.

I began to think it all through again. What the hermit was saying became painfully clear: Solitude brings the raw material of life to the surface of our souls. It turns an inner light on the external chaos of our lives and requires us to come to grips with it. Then the questions speak to us loud and clear: What should I be doing that I'm not? What am I doing that should go? What sand has collected in my soul that must be dredged away? The function of a life of solitude is not protection from noise. It is eternal confrontation with the noise within us.

When we temporarily take ourselves away from the things that serve to distract us from what is going on inside of us—when we step back from the work, the children, the blaring house parties, and the rapids of daily life every once in a while—we give ourselves back to ourselves. No hermitage is necessary. There is no reason to run away. There is no call to go away forever. What is needed is honesty of heart and some kind of periodic distance from the daily that it takes to cure ourselves of the infectious diseases of a noisy and aimless life.

It was after my meeting with the hermit that an item in my journal helped me to bring both ideas together: "The process of woman's self-invention," Delores S. Williams wrote, "makes a woman real to herself." And this time I wrote,

> Things have changed for me a bit in life. I'm not completely sure why or how. All I know is that I still feel removed from everything around me but now I am very serene about it. In fact, it feels quite right. As an only child I grew up this way, now I have completed the circle: Now there is only, ironically, God and me again. What—who—can possibly hurt me?

I had finally reinvented the real me. My life is my hermitage. The quiet solitude of private space, carved out consciously and sought out often, is simply its inner sanctum.

Chapter Nine

THE SELF:
THE GROUND OF OUR BECOMING

If all the flowers wanted to be roses, nature would lose her spring-time beauty and the fields would no longer be decked out with little wild flowers.

—Thérèse of Lisieux

Being someone else is not what life is about. The question is, How can I be me, fully me, truly me? The answer comes with great pain. And the answer is "move on."

—Joan Chittister, Journal, April 24

THE LADY LOOKED AT ME WITH BARELY DISGUISED PITY. "Oh, my dear," she said, her brow wrinkled, her eyes squinting. "I'm so sorry. I had no idea you were an only child. You seem so normal." *Normal* had the ring of incredulity to it. I smiled back at her disarmingly. I had learned to smile about my disease a lot. This time I was applying for a scholarship to a summer camp. "'You must be so lonely," the lady went on.

"I like it," I said.

She blanched a bit. "Poor child," she said under her breath.

When I was young, child-rearing theory came down heavy on only children. To be an only child, the thinking ran, meant to be deprived in some way, less developed than children with siblings. They never convinced my mother that there was anything wrong with it at all. But on one point, she was crystal clear: "If anything happens to me, Joan," she would say over and over again, "there will be no one to take care of you. You have to be able to take care of yourself." I had to learn to "do things for myself," "be myself," "watch myself," "decide for myself," "handle myself." It was the ever-recurring theme while she prepared me to be alone in the world. And it wasn't all wrong.

Whatever the now-current science of personal development may theorize, the fact remains that the self is all we have. It is the raw material of the spiritual life. It is not the world with which we wrestle; it is the self that is the antagonist in our lives. The cry of the restless self is the cry for the God beyond the little gods we fashion along the way.

Self is what enables us to refuse to settle down, in love with the mediocre, satisfied with the banal, because the self is always on its way to somewhere else. Self is the seeker within. Even when we cannot be moved by the world around us, self rages on inside of us, relentless in its seeking, regardless of its restraints. We get one thing we want—and find that we want something more. We achieve what we set out to do—and find that we begin to look almost immediately for some other hill to climb.

Dissatisfaction becomes the spiritual director of our souls. We keep trying to be satisfied—accept what you have, we tell ourselves—when satisfaction may be the chloroform of life. God is life, not torpidity. "You shall worship the Sovereign your God, and God only shall you serve," my journal reminded me in Matthew, chapter 4. And I called myself on it. I wrote,

> These words trip off the tongue—all the while I worship other gods. Lesser genies of my ravenous soul. I have worshiped so many false gods in life, yet in the collapse of each of them—and they have indeed all collapsed—I have come closer, ironically, to the god who is God. Everything else has failed me—people, privilege, positions, profit—but not this God who is "not in the whirlwind." That God, like a magnet, draws me on. And someday, perhaps, I will lose myself down the black hole of nothingness and find everything. Without the dissatisfaction of the soul, how would we ever find our way to more?

The greatest spiritual problem of them all may be that we are simply too willing to give over our sense of direction, our compulsion to search, to those who want from us anything but a self. They want obedience or conformity or sacrifice and silence. They do not want us to make up our own minds about anything. They want us to put our minds down at the altar of oblivion so that systems and institutions can thrive, while the soul smothers under the weight of its own indifference. "We cannot afford not to fight for growth and understanding, even when it is painful, as it is bound to be," May Sarton had written. But even then, I was trying to deny the need to go on growing, changing, becoming. I wrote back,

> When we grow enough to understand that we are at a dead end, then what? Is it time to be resigned or time to struggle for breath, for new life, with all our might? I always thought that life got quieter, more settled, happier as time went on. But that's not true. On the contrary. We simply become

more aware of what we've missed, what we've given ourselves to that was not worth the giving.

The struggle to be fully alive is an eternal one because the growth of the self is an eternal process. We have been falsely taught, of course, that growth occurs in ironclad stages: infancy, childhood, adolescence, and then—at twenty-one—adulthood. We can almost hear the laughter in the heavens as we say it. But if we believe it as we say it, it is no wonder that we refuse to ask for help when we need it, and take advice from no one about anything, and collapse under the pressure of our failures, and feel embarrassed by our embarrassments. Once we doom ourselves to "premature adulthood," to adulthood without the experience of doubt, we are beyond help. We deny ourselves help. We refuse help. Then we muffle the restless, struggling self. The journal entry for one New Year's Day read, "Through the days to come, in every time of year or climate, may you know the luminous goodness of God, creator of all things, all people." And I wrote,

> I do not doubt the goodness of God. I do doubt my own ability, my own strength to reach out and claim it. I am too busy doing what I "should" do rather than being what I must be if I am ever to be whole, to be happy.

The longing to begin again never ceases. It eats away at us, prodding us on, cautioning us to stay. It is the yin and yang of life. Somewhere between the tug and the pull lies good sense. But when the struggle for the fullness of the self ends, we have died, whether we are buried or not. Who has not known the great desire to quit, to begin again, to be free of what is in order to be available for what could be? Crossover points are common in life. But it is not the crossing over that counts—and most of us, in fact, do not. In the long run, we stay where we are, grateful to be settled, less intent on having perfection, more wedded to familiarity than to the thought of beginning again. No, it is not the act of leaving one thing to do another that changes us. On the contrary. The very act of grappling with the desire to quit, of facing the compulsion to start over, of finding ourselves most ourselves where we are brings us to a new level of life, a new depth of heart. Then we come into our own. Then we do, indeed, begin again—but this time from the inside out, not the outside in. We don't change our circumstances; we change our attitudes. We become a self that is self-contained, not trapped.

I wrote later in response to another Scripture: "In the beginning was the Word and the Word was with God and the Word was God." My response was honest and clear—full of that same drive toward self-sufficiency that my mother had always wanted for me. It read,

> This week I will start a new book. I live in hope of the living Word in it. I also listen for the word of my own life that is true. Is it simply to go on, to finish what I began simply because I began it? Or is it to become what's missing, whatever the upheaval it will cost me. That is the major question of my life right now. I long to put down the institution, the definition, the responsibilities, the expectations, the connections. I long to begin over . . . to become silence . . . to disappear.

But here I stay because here is where the growing self remains for me still. And I know it, however much I keep wondering if it is drained of its juices. Mercy Oduyoye was quoted in the journal as saying, "When the Spirit of Truth comes we shall experience freedom, set free from all that has closed us in." And I wrote what I knew to be unalterably true:

> We are all so closed in and we don't even know it: by our language, by our cultures, by our religions, by our sex, by our age. So how can we possibly expect that we know God? I feel as if my life has been spent straining to see through a knothole the size of a pinhead into a dark room. But when we even begin to see, the breadth of the view breaks open the heart.

It is only in the excursions of the self beyond the self that we expand the view of God that draws us on. It is not a matter of going anywhere. It is all a matter of growing, of becoming the fullness of the self, exactly where we are.

Chapter 10

COMMITMENT: THE PLACE OF CHANGE IN THE SPIRITUAL LIFE

Set your minds on things that are above, not on things that are on earth.

—Colossians 3:2

All my life my mind has been "set on things that are above." And as a result, the me that is in need of freedom and life and joy and unlimited possibility and love has languished. Been ignored. Suppressed. And now, on the brink of the grave, that me is crying for attention. Is this unfinished business—or temptation? Is it an opportunity, a "call" or a snare? Is it a lesser life or the rest of life? And how will I ever know if I should have continued the journey or stay fixed in a system on the way to dust. Where are you, O God, in this?

—Joan Chittister, Journal, April 4

LOOKING OUT OVER THE ATLANTIC OCEAN YESTERDAY, the wind whipping the Irish coast, my mind blank, a ghost rose out of the sea of my life. I could see her as if she were standing in front of me, and I knew that her story, once a punctuation mark in my own life, had something to say to us all.

It was profession day in the monastery. The multiple stages of profession in pre–Vatican II religious life had all the trappings of a modern wedding and more.

In the earliest stages of commitment, the novice wore a wedding gown and received the habit and white veil. As a scholastic, at a time of first vows, the black veil. Three years later, at final profession, she received a ring. More than that, she "went under the pall," the rough black cover then used to shroud coffins in burial ceremonies, while officials of the community lit funeral candles at each point of the square to signify her death to the world.

The occasion reeked of finality, of change from one kind of person to another. This was solemn. This was final. After a ceremony like that, few women, if any, who made final profession ever left.

What I remember most about this particular profession day is not profession itself. One of the new scholastics and I had gone to high school together. We had even developed a kind of pidgin English there, as young people do to protect their private lives from the adults around them. As we left the chapel after the ceremony, I in the new white veil of a novice, she having taken first vows, she spoke to me now, not in English, but in the old second language we'd created for ourselves. "Joan," she said to me, her eyes watering, her back rigid, "I have just made the mistake of my life."

Twelve years passed. Then, emotionally exhausted and socially frazzled from trying to do what went constantly against the grain of her soul—final vows or no final vows— she finally left the monastery. The community was shocked, even scandalized, perhaps. And I should have been, too, I suppose. But I wasn't. On the contrary, I breathed a sigh of relief for her.

I learned a great deal about commitment that day, but not what people would imagine, I'm sure. I learned that her story is a commitment story. I would argue later that by leaving the community, she didn't break a commitment; she honored it.

In order to understand the nature of commitment, there are two questions that need to be asked about it. The first is, When does it happen? The second is, What is it about? The answers are more obvious than we have been given to believe.

First, commitment happens on a daily basis, not once and forever. It is something we grow into, not something we come to full-blown. And second, it is not a call to some sort of static state of life. It is a call to move always toward the best self we can possibly be.

The prompt in my idea-journal read one day, "But Jesus came and touched them, saying, 'Rise and have no fear.'" Reading it a few years later, my response surprised even me. I wrote,

> I wonder what it takes to really "rise and have no fear"? I have a great deal of fear sometimes. I fear that I will do poorly what I want to do well. I fear that I have done all the wrong things in life, made all the wrong choices. I fear being trapped by other people's expectations. I fear grinding my life away in the great institutional sacrifice—for which there is no final sense, and even little present purpose. I watch religious life and fear that it was the wrong thing to have done in the first place and yet—even knowing how poorly I've done it—I know it was not. And in the core of me, as a result, I really do "have no fear."

Commitment, I had finally come to understand, drives us on past the pursuit of perfection to a sense of being at home within ourselves.

Commitment is what we have at the end of a hectic day, after the children have finally gone to sleep, and we know that, hard as it is, staying here, loving these children, paying these bills, is still what we must do if we are to be who we really want to be. When we revisit an old decision and know, whatever the scars of it, that this way of life is still the best thing we could have done for ourselves to become the spiritual fullness of what we are capable of being, we are at last "committed."

At the same time, commitment has its problems—and its distortions. One kind of spiritual culture says that once you've begun a thing, you must complete it, no matter the cost. The other culture says that once a thing begins to get difficult, happiness—fulfillment—demands that we leave it and start over somewhere else, whatever the effect on everyone around us. One posture glorifies masochism; the other, license. I understand both positions, but I have come to deny both of them.

The journal entry from Celia Allison Hahn made me think consciously about both self-sacrifice and self-fulfillment. Hahn wrote, "As men and women weigh intimacy against responsibility, they discover that they have brought different weights and measurements to the task." Clearly Hahn was talking about the difference in gender orientations toward responsibility and intimacy, but I thought of it more broadly than that. I wrote,

> More people stay in marriages out of a sense of responsibility than of intimacy, I'm sure. And isn't that why I stay where I stay, too? The more intimate I have become with God, the less dependent I feel on the community for personal satisfaction or security, as if the dailiness of personal connections are now secondary to the Center of the life. So

I am not here because I so much need these particular people but because I must meet the responsibilities of the years.

There is a point of personal growth, in other words, at which I become myself, become free, become open to the world. Then commitment has done its thing. Then I do not stay where I am because I must. I stay where I am because where I am has brought me to a point of concern beyond the self. There are "the responsibilities of the years," those obligations that emerge from the awareness of my place in the world. Then I know that it is not only right for me, but it is also right for others, that I am there. I am where I am supposed to be, not only for my own development, but for the sake of the development of the world around me.

But "right" as a thing may be for me, the temptation to abandon it tests our inner direction every day. Test is the price of commitment. "Looking, listening, and learning offer the modern equivalent of moving through life as a pilgrimage," Mary Catherine Bateson wrote. And I wrote back on one particularly difficult day, it seems,

> My "pilgrimage" has been a different one. For me, it has been listening, learning, and saying. The end of this compulsion to truth is unclear to me. Will it be silence, alienation, or abandonment? Will I remain in this holy vessel of endless sin and sexism called the church? Or will I choose to follow my own sins instead? It is a more profound question than first meets the eye.

Commitment has something to do with seeing a good thing through—even when it goes bad in places. It lies in working out my own weaknesses, even as I work out the weaknesses around me. It unmasks me to myself. Commitment gives me the chance to stay in place and grow. It is not about staying in place and going to seed.

"Those who find their life will lose it, and those who lose their life for my sake will find it," my journal quoted Matthew 10. This time I wrote in response,

> Whatever we do, we do for a purpose larger than ourselves or there is no use doing it at all. The real purpose of our lives is not for ourselves alone. It is to co-create the world. It is to bring the rest of the world to the point of humanity we think ourselves to have achieved. It is when all I care about is my life that I begin to have it seep out of me into a pool of selfishness so deep that I miss the juice of all the life that is around me.

Commitment does not end at its beginning. It is the vehicle by which we unfold before ourselves and the world into something worth being at the end of it: a loving father, a good mother, a faithful religious, a deeply spirit-filled human being whose presence is a gift to the world. But getting there may take a lot of changing until we come to that place that does not bind the spirit and serves to unleash the energy of the soul. To find in ourselves our deepest aspirations is to discover whether the path to God is either still before us to be seized or yet behind us, prodding us on.

I have no idea what happened to the sister who knew the day she took her vows that she was in the wrong place to become what she needed to become in life. But I can tell you this: She may have known more about commitment that day than any of the rest of us did.

Balance: Going through Life Whole and Holy

Reflect on your times of busyness and preoccupation, times when you possibly resist God's presence.

—Wendy Miller

I am never closer to God than in the moments when I am busiest. It is in those times that I throw myself on the mind of God and listen to know if the direction is right, if the words are right, if the ideas are right. Then God becomes the radar by which I steer. I stray farthest from the consciousness of God when I relax and coast. Then I take God for granted.

—Joan Chittister, Journal, July 12

I WROTE, "I AM NEVER CLOSER TO GOD THAN IN THE moments when I am busiest" in great sincerity. But that doesn't mean that it's always true. Sometimes I forget that busyness, too, can be a bridge to God. Busyness requires its own kind of spiritual discipline and practice.

When we left Wisconsin at 4:30 p.m., the weather was cold, clear, crisp. It was a short flight. In one hour I'd be in Minneapolis; in another two, I'd be in Pittsburgh. I breathed a sigh of relief. I'd get to the motel early enough to get a good night's sleep before the next set of meetings began the following morning.

But, in Minneapolis, they posted the flight as delayed for an hour. Cell phones came out all over the boarding area.

Two hours later, they posted another delay. People crowded the desk in an attempt to make new connections.

An hour after that, they moved us out of one boarding area to another a good half-mile away. One man swore at the gate agent; a woman demanded that they send a porter to help her move.

At midnight, they apologized a third time. They were going to send up new equipment. They just weren't sure how long it would take to get it here. People swarmed the desk to get hotel and breakfast vouchers.

At 1:00 a.m. they told us the problem was now lack of crew. At 2:30 a.m. flight attendants finally arrived. At 5:00 a.m., thirteen hours after I left Grand Rapids, I walked into the motel in Pittsburgh. Eight hours late. I was bone tired, up-tight, and hungry. Was any amount of business, any kind of meeting, worth it? And what could I do about it anyway? All the schedules were set. All the commitments were long made.

It occurred to me that life made more sense before the invention of the lightbulb. Or, let's put it this way, before the lightbulb came along, good sense was more a way of life than it was a virtue. Without lightbulbs there were only so many things you could do in a day and for only so much time. When night came—at some seasons of the year as early as four o'clock in the afternoon—you had to stop, take stock, sit in front of the fire, or sleep until the light returned. Now, the world as we know it stays awake twenty-four hours a day, watches television twenty-four hours a day, works twenty-four hours a day, eats twenty-four hours a day, parties twenty-four hours a day, moves twenty-four hours a day. Now, there is nothing that cannot be done to excess.

Balance—physical, social, and emotional—is at a premium. What we forget is that a lack of personal balance brings with it high spiritual costs, as well. "Take my yoke upon you," my journal reminded me from Matthew, "and learn from me for I am gentle and lowly of heart and you will find rest for your souls." I had known too many long nights, canceled meetings, and bad speaking situations not to recognize the spiritual disease that lack of balance brings. I responded,

> The message is a clear one: being gentle and humble is a spiritual posture that is good for mental health. When I am given to anger or driven by the kind of pride that fears failure and resists defeat, I doom myself to eternal agitation. I manufacture my own anguish. When I demand that the world take the shape I decide for it, when I get frustrated at airline counters and impatient with my computer, I insist on waging eternal contest with life. Then I have the nerve to wonder how the world got dedicated to violence? Then I wonder why I have no peace. The truth is that the upheavals all started with me. The spiritual equation is obvious: exterior calm leads to internal quiet.

The spiritual needs of the modern world have shifted with the changes in modern life itself. Quiet is a thing of the past. Calm is suspect. Agitation is the order of the day. Attention to beauty, reflection on ideas—on life—have little or no place in a teeming, seething, mobile world. Contemplation is in danger of being lost.

"I believe in holiness. I experience it whenever I really compose, whenever I play," the musician Marge Piercy wrote in the journal. Laid bare here for all of us to deal with was the notion that busyness could be a bridge to higher consciousness. If we allow ourselves to let one become the other. Here was a woman whose "busyness" was her spiritual life. It made sense. I knew that writing was that for me. And children were that for Mary Lou. And gardening was that for Mary. And problem solving at her computer was that for Maureen. All of those things brought each of us differently to experience that moment of integration between what we are meant to be—co-creators of the world—and what we do. They were times of immersion, times when the creator breathed in us, hovered closer than usual, moved through us. They were times of balance. I could feel the very subtle, but very real, shift in the definition. For too long holiness has been an exercise, rather than a state of mind. I wrote in reply,

> I don't know what holiness is anymore but I doubt that it is rule-keeping, because nobody does. We each simply stumble through our humanity, having come out of nowhere and going back to the same place. In between the two end points is survival. Maybe sanity is holiness, the ability to endure with equanimity what cannot be avoided—the trust that there must be more than this jangle of things we call life.

The spiritual life opens us to a world beyond cacophony. In the spiritual life lies the center of balance in us. Once balanced in God we become balanced in ourselves. Once we steep ourselves in a sense of rightness in the universe, we find ourselves on friendly terms with it. When we realize that there is a Cosmic Heart that wishes us well and has provided for our needs, if we can only control them, all of life becomes more a spiritual experience than an irritation. It is a matter of learning to let go, to step into the tide of life and believe in it.

When we stop demanding that the universe bow to us and we learn to bow to the universe instead, holiness sets in. The journal quoted the Epistle to the Romans this time: "Some people esteem one day as better than another," it said, "while others esteem all days alike. Let all be fully convinced in their own mind." After years of struggling with my own frustrations, I could write this time,

> Life is a matter of attitude. It becomes what we bring to it. I find myself vacillating between the very poles Paul describes. At pole one, I take the position that this particular thing is good but this other thing is bad. So my days are either wonderful or terrible depending on whether they take the shape I will for them. At pole two, I take the position that everything that happens is life-giving somehow, even when I can't see how. Then God is in the crevices where I never thought to look. "Make up your mind," Paul seems to say, "and it will change your whole life."

The quality of life is in our own hands. But shaping it takes a spirituality of balance. "We should be peaceful in our words and deeds and in our way of life," Angela Foligno wrote. It was ancient spirituality, tried and true. And I understood it in a whole new way. I wrote,

> It's so true. Peace is a choice. If I didn't worry, didn't fear, didn't react negatively to things, I wouldn't be disturbed by them. But that's Buddhist, they tell me. Am I Buddhist, too? As well as Jewish. As well as Catholic. I hope so. I want to live life and know God in every possible way.

Chapter Twelve

DARKNESS:
A WAY TO THE LIGHT

Embracing honesty regarding our physical selves allows us to pierce the surface and reach our deeper spiritual selves.

—Maria Harris

My physical self is only reflecting the condition of my soul. I've lost the spring in my step, my clothes look terrible, I've put on weight, my color is grey. My heart is showing in my body. Everything is going well but me. The work sustains me but life is a cage rather than a possibility. Surely somewhere in this cave there is a light. But where is it? When will it shine again? What is it?

—Joan Chittister, Journal, April 8

FAITH AND LIFE HAVE A WAY OF GETTING ALL MIXED UP together. When life goes sour, we blame God. Or worse, we abandon the God who sustains us in life, as if what has happened to us is God's fault. We forget then that without God we would never survive it at all. We sink into our little daily depressions and call our lot unbearable. We fail to take hold of where we are, to deal with life for ourselves. We stew in the juices of yesterday. I ought to know; I've done it time and time again.

I was a young sister the first time it happened. After three years of formation, I had settled into the monastery like a mole in a tunnel. While other people my age were getting married, having children, struggling to find jobs, going into large debts to buy small houses, the biggest problem I faced every day was getting to and from college. Life was neat. I went to prayer, went to classes, did various work rotations in the community, like table waiting or sweeping halls, and got to bed early at night. From some perspectives, it could have looked like the ideal monastic life. From another angle, it was lifelessness at its ultimate.

Everything in my life was safe and familiar. It suited me perfectly. Little did I know that if I was dealing with any problem at all at that stage of life, it was the malignancy of routine.

Then, one day they decided to send me down diocese to a small rural school where I would teach double grades. I broke out into hives. But the delaying tactic, subconscious as it may have been, didn't work, thank God. They sent me anyway. They broadened my world. They plunged me into exactly what I did not want to do. It was sink or swim time, and I survived. But not only survived. I learned that the gift of life comes just where we think death for us must surely be. Then, we become the more of ourselves.

But even so, reluctance to change has been the scourge of my life. Years later, in fact, my journal recorded an idea from Rosellen Brown. She wrote, "Do I repeat an experience and deepen into it or do I go somewhere else, indulge my curiosity, learn another way?" I responded to that idea with this one:

I am a person who puts down deep roots, the tearing up of which is a rending, wrenching thing. I have never been able to move on easily. And yet now, at this stage of life, I feel as if I could simply walk off the edge of the world and never look back. I could go on alone in bliss . . . and why don't I? Because I put down deep, deep roots.

We learn faith very slowly. At least I did. It took a whole series of changes before I got the message that God is in the next place as surely as God is in this one. However successful every transition in my life has ever been—and there have been lots of them—I have dug in my heels to resist the very thought of another one. I put down roots into the earth of my comfort zone and refused to move into the light.

I had weathered the death of one father, deep religious struggles with another one, the long battle back from paralysis, thirteen years of teaching, and life change after life change after life change. But it was years before I figured out how change and failure were among the best friends of the soul.

The spiritual life does not come cheap. It is not a stroll down a Mary Poppins path with a candy-store God who gives sweets and miracles. It is a walk into the dark with the God who is the light that leads us through darkness.

Darkness, I have discovered, is the way we come to see. It creates the depressions that, once faced, teach us to trust. It gives us the sensitivity it takes to understand the depth of the pain in others. It seeds in us the humility it takes to learn to live gently with the rest of the universe. It opens us to new possibilities within ourselves.

Darkness is a very spiritual thing.

My spiritual journal challenged me one day to think about the nature of suffering and its place in the spiritual life. Myra B. Nagel had written, "The season of Lent is a time to reflect on the cross and its meaning for our lives." I reflected,

> There is no doubt in my mind that the cross is significant in any life. Who ever carries a cross and is the same at the end of the journey as they were at the beginning? The only question is the nature of the change. I have so far always been stronger at the end of struggle than I was at the outset. But I have always been more independent, distant, isolated, as well. That hasn't been all bad—but it has, at the same time, taken its toll.

I have discovered over time that the cross is supposed to take its toll on us. It forms us to find God in the shadows of life. Ironically enough, it is the cross that teaches us hope. When we have survived our own cross, risen alive from the grave of its despair, we begin to know that we can survive again and again and again, whatever life sends us in the future. It is this hope that carries us from stage to stage in life, singing and dancing around dark corners.

But hope is not a private virtue. Hope makes us witness to the invincibility of the spirit. The hope we bring to the other becomes the one sure gift we have to give to those in pain. What's more, having suffered ourselves, we become more caring toward those in darknesses of their own. Suffering is what turns us into caring people.

Then, after we have survived the first injustice, the first loss, the first fear, the first insecurity, suffering brings more than hope. It brings patience and surety as well. Suffering teaches us to wait and to believe that the end of this tunnel is toward the light. The journal quoted Scripture, Romans 8:25: "But if we hope for what we do not see, we wait for it with patience." By that time I had apparently suffered enough to be able to write back from a bedrock of hope myself,

> Of course I hope for what I do not see: I do not see God's justice fulfilled, God's equality mirrored, God's Spirit recognized, heard, honored in everyone—even in the church. But I wait in hope for what I know must be. It's not if these things will come that I'm about in life. It's when. And no, I don't know when but I do know for sure that it will. Why? Because this God wills for us "our weal and not our woe."

I had a lifetime of experience to prove it. My father's death at twenty-three did not destroy my twenty-one-year-old mother. Years of uncertainty and family tension did not dash my hope that resolution was possible and conflict was creative. Formation in a life geared to withdrawal and dependence had not damped my vision of personal responsibility for a world in pain. On the contrary, personal suffering stretches us beyond ourselves to the pain of the world.

Even as a community we learned the link between personal suffering and the pain of the world—as most families do. The community itself had faced bankruptcy, the loss of the monastery, eviction from the land, interruption of programs and education and the normal processes of professional development. Now we understood the fears of homelessness and loss and hunger and deprivation ourselves in ways no books could teach us. Like everyone else in the world, we discovered that suffering sharpens our awareness of others in a way nothing else can. Then suffering leads us to be poor with the poor, to be oppressed with the oppressed, to be ready to lift up those around us like poor Amish raise barns for other Amish as poor as themselves. But to do that, we must go beyond ourselves.

93

We must reach out beyond our own pain. We must see ourselves as ambassadors of understanding. We suffer in order to become the presence of God ourselves. The journal carried an excerpt from Sallie McFague: "We ask God, as one would a friend to be present in the joy of our shared meals and in the suffering of strangers." And I knew the implications of the statement. I wrote back,

> I have just finished a week at Chautauqua talking about the God at work in us. And I have done so little myself to be that godliness to the poor, to the refugee, to the church that is rigid and harsh. I know the things that must be done but I myself do not do them. I love the safe and comfortable. I do not seek the risk of revolution.

Yet the revolution starts in my own openness to change, to others, to the possible, to the difficult. I tell myself that that is someone else's problem, someone else's gift, someone else's call. I tell myself anything it takes to avoid another major change in my own life.

I have decided that security is my sin but not only my sin. We humans cling like barnacles to yesterday as if heaven were behind us rather than ahead. We measure all good by the good we have today. We allow our little successes to dominate our vision. We fail to see that more is possible. We make ourselves God and wonder why we don't recognize God when the God of conversion comes again to stretch our souls. We take the past as our standard and run the risk of being smothered by it in our tracks.

The God of the Dance beckons us out of the caves of the soul to faith and trust and new beginnings. But we prefer the dark. We miss the holy-making mystery of the dark. We avoid the holy demands that darkness brings and allow it instead to decay into depression. My journal was clear: "Somehow we need to retain what is valuable from the past and move with courage and vigor into the future," Jean Blomquist wrote. I responded,

> It's when we get trapped in the past—in its details, and its shame, and its narrow boxes and short leashes—that life stops for us. When life is defined for us by others, we limit our sense of ourselves. Then we dismiss the God of Possibility from our lives. We refuse to become the more that we are. We sit on the dung heap of our past and make it our present. We fail to believe that God is. That God is in us. That God is calling us out of the darkness into the light.

Darkness is one of the ways to God, provided we see it as leading to the light. Provided we don't turn it into the death of our own soul.

IMMERSION IN LIFE: THE OTHER SIDE OF INWARDNESS

Teach us to listen to the stirring of our own longing for there we will discover you again.

—Sharon Thornton

It is a wonderful moment in the spiritual life when we come to re-alize that the experience of longing for something is not evil, not "sin," not selfishness. It is the voice of God leading us to discover new parts of creation in ourselves—new experience of creation everywhere. We have been taught to fear desire rather than to reflect on it as the lodestone of the heart. How sad.

—Joan Chittister, Journal, January 8

IT IS SO EASY TO ESCAPE INTO THE SELF AND CALL THE escape holiness. There are whole streams of the spiritual tradition—spawned by Plato's Theory of Forms, en-shrined by the Manichees in a spirituality of negation, bol-stered by Augustine's theory of original sin—which required the rejection of the world as an element of the spiritual life. So much for the Jesus who became flesh. So much for a positive theology of creation. So much for the body as vehicle of the spirit.

A theology of negation may look suspect now in a cul-ture of creature comforts. It may even seem groundless in a scientific world enthralled by the wonders of the human body, miracles of creation, a technology of possibility, and newfound respect for nature. But it thrived in earlier ages. And it did untold amounts of damage. Not only to the body itself, but to the spirit as well. It made all of life suspect: We learned to fear relationships and joy and comfort and sex and the senses and sweet life anywhere and everywhere we found it. We went through life missing it. To be holy meant to leave the world. To be worldly was the worst kind of fault.

I remember a conversation that made the tension all too obvious to me. Women religious had been in the process of changing from medieval habits to contemporary clothes for about a year when it happened. I found myself in an elevator with a charming middle-aged man who made interesting conversation for fifty floors.

"And what do you do, young lady?" the man said, as we reached the lobby.

"I'm a Benedictine sister," I said quite easily.

His face changed; his brow furrowed. When the elevator door slid open, he stood there for a moment blocking it. "Do you realize," he said, turning around to face me head on, embarrassed at himself, even more angry at me, "I could have made a pass at you? Why aren't you in a habit?"

I looked him straight in the eye: "And what difference does a habit make?" I asked him. "Are you married? And if you are, why would you be making a pass at anyone at all? And if you aren't, why would you treat a strange woman as if she were an object for your consumption?"

He stalked across the lobby and never looked back. I couldn't help but think of all the women who had been raped and all the men who went free of the charges because "of what the women were wearing." The length of a woman's skirt had become an object of morality just as great or even greater than the immorality itself.

We made the body an enemy. The physical life came to be regarded as some kind of bastard child of creation. Holiness required an excursion into repression of everything godly on earth. Willingness to abuse the self, to punish it and repress it and deny it, had become the measure of sanctity. The normal became abnormal.

This division of life into realms of the sacred and the secular has divided us against ourselves. It has blocked our experience of the divine in the human. It has divinized some categories of the natural—made some things holy that are not, like clerical functionaries or instruments of liturgy—and made the rest of the natural dangerous, if not obscene.

Years after the conversation in the elevator, my journal indicated the effects of it all. Trish Herbert had written, "You can't teach a person anything. You can create an environment in which the person can look within, unlocking the treasures of the past and discovering the wisdom there." After years of symbolic asceticism—years of fasting and silence and permissions, all designed to bring us to a kind of quality-controlled perfection—I wrote in return,

> Life is one long learning process never achieved, never accomplished. We grew up thinking we were going toward "perfection." Now we know that perfection does not even exist, is always changing, is forever somewhere and something else. Is that all there is to learn? Maybe that is enough.

Nevertheless, learning that we cannot ever achieve perfection in this life does not come easily in a spiritual climate based on perfection. The spirituality of perfection is a spirituality of failure. What we need is a spirituality of growth. We go through life choosing good from better, bad from good, better from best. Every twist of life becomes another learning, another opportunity to take a higher road than the one we took before it, true. But it is also a pilgrimage into ever more serious understandings.

We learn, for instance, that cloister and contemplation are not synonyms. For some people, cloister leads to contemplation. For others the face of God is on every face they see. Contemplatives do not hide from life. They don't fear the natural. They experience the touch of God through everything in life. Life itself consumes them with a sense of the sacred everywhere.

It is not necessary to withdraw from the world in order to be holy. In fact, it may be more difficult to make a spiritual case for withdrawal than it is to understand creative immersion in the world around us. Otherwise, how do we explain the Jesus who walked from Galilee to Jerusalem, curing lepers, giving sight to the blind, raising women from the dead? Does Jesus qualify as a contemplative or not? And if so, then surely withdrawal is not the only way to get to be one.

We must learn that life itself is of God, that the natural is sacred, and that an inward life and immersion in life are of a piece. If we are in God, then all of life becomes sacred to us. To seek God means to find God around us. The God-questions propel us into life, in fact. It is precisely when we begin to see the world through the eyes of God that life becomes the measure of our own godliness. Then life becomes the stuff of holiness for us, not a spiritual threat. Human life becomes the eternal life of the spirit. "If every day is an awakening, you will never grow old. You will just keep growing," Gail Sheehy wrote. But I wrote back, after years of experience, a lifetime of search marked by a lifetime of holy failures,

> Well, it is true, I think, that every day we grow—but I am not so certain that every day is an awakening. Sometimes we grow in silent places that do not burst through to daylight and voice for years. Sometimes we wake up and reach back and know newly, finally, what we thought we knew or did not want to know years before. That's the real awakening.

To awaken, to grow, we must be fully engaged in the process of living. It is from life that we learn to learn—and learn to begin again. It is the way we go through life—dealing with others, absorbing the natural, dealing with difficulties, inebriated by beauty, burned by our excesses, addicted to one nothingness after another, open to newness—that makes us human enough to grow into the divine. It is from life that we learn to know God and strive for godliness.

It is the choices we make every day of our lives, either to grow or to stagnate, that determine the depth of our soul. "I believe we each choose our journey and discover what life is about in our own way," Jody Miller Stevenson wrote. I responded to the statement with the surety of one who has learned the truth of a thing the hard way. As we all do. I wrote,

> Choice is a very strange thing. We so often choose what we know—our context limits our options—and then later we discover more. What happens then? Can we choose again? Only with wrenching. Only with pain. No, I am not sure we really choose as freely as we like to think. But I am sure that in the choices we do make that we "discover what life is about." Some of it is barely bearable; some of it is joyful where we would never have expected it to be.

And all of it is the stuff of holiness. None of it is to be excluded. It is finding God through baptism by life that is the real gauge of our inwardness. Pity those whose holiness is made of less.

Chapter Thirteen

RELATIONSHIPS:
TO KNOW AND BE KNOWN

*What is essential for taking back a yesterday is understanding that
you are not alone, even in the wilderness.*

—Linda H. Hollies

*Knowing that someone else knows where you are, feels the way you
feel, does—for me at least—really "take back yesterday." It smooths
whatever scars were suffered there. It is being alone in my pain, my
fear, the burden of my memories, that presses my face to the ground.
But when one person says, "I know,"...."I understand,"...."I can
see why you feel that way," I become whole again. Sane. Mature. It
is the humanity of the other that brings my humanity back to life.*

—Joan Chittister, Journal, February 20

WE GROW UP TALKING ABOUT HUMAN RELATIONSHIPS
and reading poetry that says "No man is an island." But for
far too long, those ideas have had a way of staying strangely
disembodied. The love that is love passed us by in favor of
love that was more intellectual than real. Even marriage was
treated as domestic arrangement—the "natural" thing to
do—or as some kind of spiritual deterrent—as in, a better

103

thing to do than to "burn." The idea that marriage might be the way God broke into lives meant to be godly for one another escaped us. The whole notion that marriage gave us an idea of God's love for us approached the blasphemous.

We knew, of course, that human relationships had something to do with "loving my neighbor as myself." The simplest understanding of Christianity, they told us, required that we reach out to others. We were all children of God, after all, so we were responsible for one another. But I did not know that relationship itself tested that theory. Being responsible for the other, if we could not form real relationships, approached the impossible. To give love a person needs to have known love, needs to realize that love is the only real happiness we need—which is why so many children raised in monstrous, loveless conditions become monsters.

No one said those things much. Instead we got the idea that love came in pallid packages. The more pallid, the better. We were not told that human love incarnated the divine. On the contrary, what we did know, given the long tradition of suspicion that surrounded human love in the Jansenistic West, was that really holy people did well to do without it. The denial of pleasure and the linking of sin to sexuality had done its work well.

Community and family and "love of neighbor" were praised, of course. They even became standards of human decency. And why not? They required benevolence, not passion. They kept us from giving in to the selfishness that characterized humanity. They cemented the human community. In fact, sheer utilitarianism, if nothing else, demanded it: I would help another, then—God forbid—if I ever needed help myself, they would help me. There was no investment of the self here. Not the real self. Christian love wanted humanitarianism, not hot-bloodedness.

But if the Christian idealization—or more to the point, disembodiment—of love was obvious, the achievement of it eluded us on all fronts. Our institutional ideals everywhere militated against it. The ideal in public life, too, was "rugged individualism," that great American can-do attitude that makes loners of us all. And, interestingly enough, even in the spiritual life, the paragon was the person for whom God alone was enough. Get holy enough, really holy, meaning celibate, and feelings were a thing of the past apparently. Great towering theologies of *Agape*—human benevolence, and *Eros*—carnal love—waged war together. One was Christian, agape, a kind of plastic kindness, and the other, Eros, was . . . well, beautiful, but lamentable. This one, the kind with tears, was the lesser kind, of course. Asceticism, the denial of the self, the denial of emotions, trapped us inside ourselves. And all for the love of God.

"Sisters and priests [religious professionals, in other words] never cry at funerals," my mother told me once. "They aren't sad that a person has died, because they know the person is now with God." Even when I was a youngster, the idea stopped me cold. This strange mixture of stoicism and spirituality jangled in my head. Did these holy people really mean "Love one another" or not, I wondered. And what kind of love was it that functioned without feelings? I had a parakeet I loved more, it seemed to me, than these Christians loved one another.

I tried to imagine not being sad if Grandma died. But I could neither picture it in my mind nor manage it when it happened. Sixteen years old at the time, I cried for days. Somehow or other, I had missed out on the spirituality of self-sufficiency, the virtue of detachment. I loved, and I hurt, and I cared. Dangerous.

And try as I might, I have never given it up. Both parents are gone now, and nothing fills the gap. Two friends I counted on went too quickly and left me wanting. In every case, the pain is welcome, and the ache is real. Better the hurt than a vapid detachment. My journal prompted me with a quotation from Jean Blomquist: "Those who guide us up, over and around the boulders and chasms of our lives reveal the many faces of God." I had known the life-giving power of love, and I wrote back without blinking,

> In fact, Jean Blomquist, do we really "see" God anywhere else in any other way? My life is one long parade of faces— but almost entirely only of those who loved me and carried me beyond the trauma of violence, beyond pain to joy—the downright adulterous joy of going beyond what threatened to destroy us and coming out the other side a full human being. The list is long but some stand out: Sister Patricia Maria, Mary Jude, Theo, Mary Michael, Maureen and Lou. I thank God that I was never seduced by "detachment."

Whatever the theory, after years of monastic life— community life—I began to see it all with a different eye. Detachment—in the sense of being emotionally unresponsive— simply did not work. When Sister Pierre died, I saw the most ascetic of our old sisters be unabashedly sad. When Ellen and Mary Bernard, young artists and blood sisters, as well as members of the community, were killed with their parents in an automobile accident, the prioress was crying too hard to make the announcement over the community's public address system. Then, at the funeral, the rest of us walked down the aisle behind the casket too blinded by tears to see our way. I got the idea that those who invest themselves in God also invested themselves in others. So much for agape, that heady, unfazed, unattached poor excuse for human bondedness.

The notion that holiness demanded emotional anemia simply did not stand up to daily scrutiny. The notion that nothing in life should engage us enough to chain our hearts to earth cried to heaven for redress. To go through life heartless is to fail to go through life at all.

We are put here to love, not for the sake of the other alone, but for our own sakes as well. To dare to love another as a person, rather than as an idea, is to turn ourselves over to be shaped and reshaped in life. The people who love us do for us what we cannot do for ourselves. They release the best in us; they shoulder us through the rough times in life; they stretch us beyond the confines of our own experiences to wider visions, to truer vistas. They show us the face of our creating, caring God on earth. I became as sure of that as I was sure of life itself. "When we are mirrored in the eyes of someone who loves us and accepts us in our essence, our soul is released," Marion Woodman wrote. And I answered her,

> I have no doubt whatsoever that being loved by someone is what gives us the ground we need from which to launch our lives beyond their small arenas. Because people believed in me, encouraged me even when they didn't really understand what I was doing, I was able to take a fateful step beyond classrooms, beyond the community, even beyond what was thought to be proper to a nun. Fateful. And fulfilling.

Perhaps the deepest spiritual understanding we can muster here is that human love is the only proof we have of the love of God. It is also the only arms God has with which to love us here and now, clearly and warmly, joyfully and achingly. Asceticism that drives love—genuine human attachment—out of us in the name of God leaves us with love without loving. Then, as spiritual people whose spirits have died within us, we never come to know the meaning of tears,

or the costs of loss, or the assurance of care, or the oppres-
siveness of pain. As Frances Young wrote, "The capacity to
give one's attention to a sufferer is a very rare and difficult
thing; it is almost a miracle; it is a miracle." And because I
had been raised to suspect feelings, mine for love and others
for pain, I could write back,

> It is so difficult to see beyond our own sufferings. I some-
> times wonder if there really is such a thing as "altruism."
> For the saints maybe. I know that I get far too much sat-
> isfaction out of what I do to call it "sacrifice" or real
> commitment to those who are suffering. But maybe some-
> day, before I die, God will grant me the grace of real un-
> selfishness—at least once.

But that, I am sure, comes only out of a heart forged by love.

Love is important to the world, to the human soul, for
more reasons than simply because it calls us out of ourselves
or is itself a sign of the love of God. Love glues the world
back together when it breaks itself apart. Only love enables
us to forgive.

When distance and detachment are the ideal, when love
is more pious platitude than real, forgiveness becomes an exercise in theological pedantry. We are told to forgive the one
who has harmed us, while our heart is still bruised and our
feelings have gone to acid. So we say the words, but we do
not feel the feelings. Or, worse, we feel feelings that are
themselves part of the pain: anger, rejection, humiliation,
abandonment, hatred even.

After years of a good relationship that had vanished
suddenly—without accusation, without explanation, with
no particular incident to justify a major breach in the relationship—I decided to deal with the situation directly. No
more casual notes, no more third-party messages, no more

dead-end telephone calls in the hope of renewing the bonds. This time I simply asked outright what I had done that could possibly have ruptured something so apparently long-standing and true. If I knew, I said, I would try with all my heart to make the reparation needed, so that we could be ourselves again. Whatever it was, I said, forgive me because it was not conscious, and I did not mean it. The conversation went well, I thought. My hopes soared. I got a good reception—on the spot. But nothing more of personal communication ever followed. Nothing. I knew then that whatever had happened—if indeed something had—was not the problem. The problem was that there had never been any love there to begin with. Only I had never realized it.

Only love enables us to forgive. The awareness that the relationship we had thought existed between us and a long-time friend no longer existed, perhaps never really had, shocks us to the center of our souls. But the shock is worth the information. Then, all that is left to know about forgiveness is that we only hurt ourselves when we refuse to let go of the pain, are not willing to go on somewhere else in life, are unable to trust again. Then, the acid inside ourselves corrodes our very souls. Better to have love enough ourselves to forgive the emotional damage that comes with abandonment than to poison our own souls with the venom of recrimination.

Only if there is love in us great enough to transcend deep hurt, great betrayal, uncaring withdrawal, can we possibly really forgive. Only if we can care for another enough to try to understand what drove the behavior that hurt us so, can we put our own pain down long enough to forgive. Forgive is what we do when our love is as real as our pain.

If we love, we can forgive anything. Which is why parents do not disown their straying children, and friends wait patiently for the healing to come that will repair the rift between them, and lovers renegotiate their marriages from one stage to another, whatever the pressures in between. Oh, yes, true—sometimes the relationship is not the same again after the rupture occurs. But that is not the point. The point is simply whether we have ever really loved well enough to forgive. To be able to forgive the other is the only sure glimpse we ever get into the love of God for us.

Only love puts the human community back together again after our humanity has torn it apart. "To forgive is not to forget, but rather to re-member whatever has been dis-membered," Carter Heyward wrote. Immersed for long years in what they told us was the glory of not loving, I wrote back my own lifetime of learnings:

> My problem does not lie in not forgiving. I can, eventually, put a thing down, make room in my heart for someone else's pressures, know that "they know not what they do." But my problem is always re-membering a broken thing. I find it al-most impossible to put the thing back together again. I take my only-child self back again to the only refuge I really trust: me.

Without human relationships that are real, based on feelings and not on clichés about the love of God, we can never understand the love of God. Then we can talk about love and never have either the inconveniences or challenges of doing it. Then we can stay in our acerbic little selves and never feel the responsibilities of feeling. Then we make love the problem and not the answer.

Chapter Fourteen

FRIENDSHIP:
THE GIFT OF INDEPENDENCE

Teach us the freedom of risking our individualism to join the circle of your family and make it complete.

—Sonya H. Chung

I want to join the human race, yes, but I do not ever again want to have my life, my ideas, my possibilities defined by an institution. I want, before I die, to know who I am when I am completely alone and perfectly free of someone else's projects, schedules, and expectations. I want to know if there is a "me" in me.

—Joan Chittister, Journal, February 6

WE GET SO ACCUSTOMED TO BEING DEFINED BY THE things and people around us, we forget how to be ourselves— if we ever knew.

When he died so suddenly, so young, the whole family took it for granted that Anne would marry again soon. She was a very youngish middle-aged woman with an impeccable taste for the well-set table, a flair for sweeping scarves and long-line coats, a love for travel and just the right touch on the arm of a man. When grief finally took its proper place in memory, she began to accept invitations again. However many couples there were in the group, friends saw to it that there would be an "extra" man there for her as the "extra" woman. A second marriage, we all decided, wouldn't be far off. It was, in fact, a tribute, people said, to the quality of the first. But Anne never did marry again. She had decided, she said, after what was clearly a near engagement had disintegrated into an on-again, off-again companionship, that she had discovered that she "liked being alone."

When Theo died everyone took special pains to make sure Alice had a steady stream of company and a series of new invitations. After all, these two women had been friends and work partners for over thirty years. Alice, older now, would surely be lonely. But she wasn't. "I don't want any new friends," she declared to a group of us one day. "Friends take too much time." I got the picture: There is a time in life when the purpose of life is to recover the self. There comes a time in life when the natural dependence of youth, disguised as companionship, wears out, and we are left with nothing except who we have become alone.

Friendship is a holy thing, but it is not an easy thing. Love and friendship take us out of ourselves, yes. And that is certainly a good thing. But if there is nothing in us that is ourselves alone, there is nothing in us to give away. Spiritual direction, "holy friendship," can be found in every great spiritual tradition. But the purpose is not to attach us to someone wiser than ourselves—the guru, the great guide, the spiritual master, the bodhisattva, the saint. The purpose of spiritual direction is to enable us to become holy ourselves. "What is the purpose of a master?" the disciple asked the Sufi. And the Sufi answered, "To make you understand the value of not having one."

Part of the process of becoming ourselves, however, lies in having someone against whose wisdom we can test our own. It lies in learning to tell our truth. "When we have friends and really share our truth with them, it changes the way things are from the inside out," Donna Schaper writes. The problem is that once we come to the point where we have a truth of our own, we have to decide when it is right, when it is safe, to share it. The struggle is a real one. I responded to the Schaper extract with caution:

> I strive for truth but never really achieve it with anyone, because I fear hurting them, disillusioning them, scandalizing them, depressing them. I would love to be "truthful" with someone but I am beginning to doubt that that's really possible for anyone. In fact, is it even fair to burden the other with a "truth" that can't be changed? Maybe the most we can achieve is honesty about our questions.

Spiritual friendship is not intended to be a crutch. It is not meant to become a substitute for self-control or the self-observation that invites us to grow. It is meant to be a bridge to the development of the self.

Friendship, the kind that develops us, enables us to carry our own burdens by helping us to understand them. It gives us the confidence to strike out on our own, as well as to share our thoughts, our concerns, with the other. Friendship enables us to become ourselves, not a duplicate—not a kind of pilot fish—of someone else.

"Friend" is a word the West uses lightly, almost without substance. In ancient Greece, friend meant political ally. Now, friend has become a synonym for companion, comrade, teammate, someone with whom we spend time. These are the people who act as a kind of social compass through our growing years. They provide a measure by which we assess ourselves: our emotional responses, our physical appearance, our intellectual acuity, our social desirability. They are a very necessary part of life. They validate us, they accompany us, they put us in touch with the world. But they do not, by and large, explore the territory of the psyche with us. We are mirror images of one another, both of us charting our way by keeping an eye on the other. They give us assurance and applause; they keep us company through the growing times; and they provide anchors for us as we settle into the self. These friends walk with us through the dips and turns of life, but these are not the people who guide our souls.

In the spiritual tradition, on the other hand, friend meant the person to whom I bared my soul, not in a gush of narcissistic self-interest, but in the way we mine for gold in rock. Carefully. Reverently. My friend is the one I see to be wiser than I. This kind of friend stands by in the midst of the spiritual whirlwind and holds out a hand on the rocks. This kind of friend offers more than presence, more than companionship. When others cling, this friend simply frees us to be ourselves. And stands by. This is the person we turn to knowing we will find unfathomed substance and understanding without evaluation. "A friend," Anne E. Carr wrote, "is one who remains fundamentally a mystery, inexhaustible, never fully known, always surprising." After years of community and friendship, I understood the implications—and the purpose of it all. I wrote,

> A friend is someone who leaves the other free. That way the mystery never ceases. I want friends who can be themselves, live their own lives, be their own persons, go their

own way—and enable me to do the same. There is something in me that wants to run through the world alone—and in that aloneness, because of that aloneness, be able to touch the whole world.

When we load the other person in a friendship, let alone in a marriage, with the obligation to satisfy all our emotional needs, we doom ourselves to disappointment. What's more, I am convinced that in the doing of that, we miss the major lesson of life: No one person can fulfill all our expectations, meet all our needs. No one and nothing here will ever be enough for us.

We thirst for something far greater than this world can satisfy. So we are always disappointed. Always. But disappointment is itself a gift. Disappointment drives our search for life. We go from one false promise to another, gobbling up things and people in great gulps only to find them go tasteless too soon. And that is the secret of contentment.

It's when we discover that enough will never be enough that we can finally stop kicking and scratching our way through life, put it all down, and let God be the point of the compass for us. Then we are ready to link arms with the rest of the human race as partners in the great enterprise of life. Then we realize not only the insufficiency of the other on whom we have put the burden of our emotional satisfaction, but of ourselves as well. Because neither we nor they are God, we can finally be gentle with one another.

Kathy Wonson Eddy wrote in the journal, "It is our center in God that gives us the impetus and energy to reach out and link with others." But I had a hard time with that one. Judging by the number of people whose hearts have been broken in their search for perfect happiness here, I have an idea that it works the other way around. I wrote,

> I have my doubts that it is "our center in God that is the impetus to reach out to others." I think it is through our linking with others that we come to know that there is "the more." We grasp for people in the hope of filling our hearts and discover only the size of the chasm they do not satisfy. Then God gets clearer and clearer.

When we finally realize that God uses beauty here to lead to the beauty that is eternal, we can allow ourselves to stop expecting it here.

Age changes the way we relate to people, as well, I think. There is a point in life when going into the self is more important than going out to the other. There is a point at which I am not seeking fun or company or approval or even wisdom anymore. I am seeking peace. I am seeking integration. I am seeking to substantiate my own identity and reset my sights. I am coming to peace with the god-self within.

Then, we begin to look to our friends for something other than guidance. We begin to look for a community of confirmation. An extract from Alice Adams read, "I think women know how to be friends. That's what saves our lives." That, I have decided, is probably true. Women bond. They don't spend their lives proving their prestige, their machismo, or their power. They need friends only to confirm the sense of personal value that comes from being listened to and from being heard, from being respected and being sought out. Friendship tells them that they are still a vital and treasured part of the human enterprise. Having watched women grow old in community, in widowhood, and in retirement for decades—and me with them, I wrote,

I don't know if women have a particular gift for friendship or not. The older I get, the richer I feel interiorly, the more I know myself to be stable and steady. So, the less I feel a need for "friends" in the old sense of the word. I do not look for a retinue of people around me to make me feel safe or loved or sure. Companions, yes, but not friends to guide me through life. Now I need them simply for conversation along the way.

The longer we stay on earth, the farther away we get from it, perhaps.

Life is a play in two acts: Birth is miracle, but the emergence of the fullness of the self is mystery. To become ourselves implies a constant struggle between two poles: dependence and independence; identification with others and self-reliance. To ignore either of these poles is to deny ourselves a necessary part of personal life and spiritual growth. On the other hand, to cultivate both means having to balance ourselves between them. It's a high-wire act of no small proportion. "Women's mysteries are of the body and the psyche," Jean Shinoda Bolen wrote. I had no doubt about the mystery of it all, though I wasn't sure that she and I would have named them the same. I saw the mystery of a woman's life as the unfathomable dance between the birthing of the self and the awe for the other. I wrote,

> The "mystery" of my life is the contradiction between a feeling of isolation on one hand and smothering on the other. In many ways, I am overly "cared for," which means constrained. In another way, I feel almost totally without real human connections or commitments. I live in "community" without the same kind of "community" that everyone else has. And yet the community does not obstruct me—and I have a wonderful life. Without them, that would be impossible. A "mystery," indeed, this balancing act between the whole and the one, the one and the whole.

To love the other without letting go of the self, to honor the fullness of the self without losing sight of the other, that is the sacrament of friendship.

In the end, friendship must be both light and liberty. "Women draw particular strength from being part of a community," Barbara Barksdale Clowse wrote. And having been part of one almost all my life, I wrote back,

> I suppose it is true that "community" is a woman's gift and strength. But for me, being able to be independent, unattached, is every bit as important. I want to know that I am not a clone. I want to know that I have come to wholeness inside myself so that I really have something to take to a community that is more than a shadow of another.

Only when we are truly ourselves can we really be any good to anybody else. Only when we are truly ourselves is our spiritual life our own.

Chapter Fifteen

LISTENING:
THE BEGINNING OF WISDOM

*Genuine wisdom involves learning from the wisdoms of other for-
gotten or overlooked people.*

—Maria Harris

*As we get older—or at least as I am getting older, more aware of
the sound of death at my back—I find myself watching other people with great intensity. I want to know what they know about living well. I want to hear from them what they now regret. I want
to sift and pan the gold of every moment that is slipping away from
me sleek and empty.*

—Joan Chittister, Journal, August 24

THE SPIRITUAL TRADITION OF THE WESTERN WORLD,
with its history of theocratic states and the subservience of
kings to popes, reeks with admonitions to obey. I asked my
novice mistress in religion class one day what a person was
supposed to do if commanded to do something he or she
felt to be wrong. She was not a bright woman, but some
things she knew without doubt: "You obey," she said. "If the
command is wrong, the person who commanded it will be

119

punished. But you will be rewarded because you obeyed." The answer convinced no one at that table.

The novice mistress's generation might still take marching orders, but ours was not so quick to defer. We were still "obedient" enough, of course—or smart enough, as the case may be—not to contest her interpretation, but we did not really accept it. We were children of the Holocaust and the Nuremberg Trials. We were young women who had watched the generation of women before us begin to come into their own during the war—and refuse to go back into domestic invisibility when it was over. We had long ago heard the word "conscience." We knew its implications. Why did the German people tolerate Hitler? Why did no Christian soldier refuse to turn on the gas jets in the crematoriums? At one level the answer is, of course, for fear of reprisal. But at another level it is just as surely the fact that obedience to authority was a cardinal virtue in that generation. Authority factored out personal conscience. Whatever we were told to do, we were taught, was God's will for us. Authority came from God to the pope to secular rulers. Our very salvation depended on obedience. So what gave the peons of society the right to resist the dictates of the state? But that thinking, later endorsed by Vatican Council II, went out with the war crimes trials. No, blind obedience held no aura for us. It may have sanctified our novice mistress's generation, but like a worm in sand, it had begun to shrivel and die in ours.

It was not obedience that was our ideal. We wanted much more than obedience. We sought wisdom, that deepdown divining rod of goodness that did not fail in the face either of authority or of license.

In my own life, I began to pay less attention to law than to the experience and insights of those around me. I looked for listeners who could help me hear my emptiness. "Associated with the feminine element in all of us is a sense of being at the core of oneself," Ann Belford Ulanov wrote. After years of looking for the truth that is deeper than law in us, I wrote back,

> The problem with being "at the core of oneself" is that we are then forced to face ourselves. There is nothing then to drown out the sense of loss or failure, aloneness or unfinishedness that the trail of life has left in us. At the core of oneself every hope is laid bare, every pain is palpable. How much easier it was when only work was the center and "obedience" was the ultimate. Now regret lurks around the frame and possibilities beckon. Too late, too late, perhaps, either to repent or to respond.

Laws and orders may constrain us but they do not shape us. Shaping happens when we meet someone whose spirit miters with the edges of our own. Customs books and canon laws didn't form me. It was the sight of Sister Margaret bent double in a pew at six o'clock in the morning and again at ten at night that opened my heart to prayer. It was Alice and her imagination that stretched my instinct to obey. To Alice anything and everything was possible. We still have the customs book she edited. "Nonsense!" she had written in the margins next to items she considered useless. It was Mary Michael and her sense of freedom that touched my heart. She walked with a lilt and talked with a twinkle in her eye and put her head back when she laughed. She made religious life human. It was Marie Claire and her largesse as local superior that years later freed the floodgates of generosity in me. "Here's money," she told us as we left for the weekend. "Stop and get something to eat on the way." Then she boomed at our backs as we left. "And don't feel obliged to spend all of it." But we did—and she never said a word, rules or no rules.

They were all little things, only inches outside the pale of the day, but they proved to me that no boundary was a barrier to life unless you allowed it to be. I was listening to the way people actually lived the life they talked about and learning that the distance between obedience and wisdom was a lifetime long. It was the accumulated experience of small acts of humanity, of strong acts of courage, of rare acts of conscience in a robotized life that changed me from an institutional martinet to a woman with a mind of her own. It was the consciences of people around me that freed me to have a conscience, as well.

"We have seen delicate flowers emerge from rocks and the hands of a little child bring healing to grief and remorse," Ansley Coe Throckmorton wrote. I thought of all the people in life who had touched my own, and I wrote,

> It is the small things in life that affect us. The great grinding machines of existence around us—the military, the banks, the institutions—control us, yes, but they do not touch us. It is at the level of the individual that we are made better, made whole. It is one nod of affirmation, one sneer that shapes us. We live in the midst of great sweeping tides of trends and fads and ideas, yes, but life becomes more and more particular as we go. We become those who have touched us.

Coming to be a person is a process, not an event. One by one, we put down the ghosts of our growing. We retreat from the absolutes on which we have been raised to test them for ourselves. We begin to listen to the self to hear what is really driving us. We listen to others now only in order to determine the quality of the moral currency we've been given. Is it true that might makes right? Is it really so that honesty is—always—the best policy? Is "change takes time" good enough? Is "because I said so" any reason to do anything? Most of all, it also means being listened to rather than being controlled, being heard rather than being suppressed.

The institutions, the systems, the governments, the authority figures—secular or sacred—that fail to listen fail to last in the long run. "Listening can be a life-giving act," Diane Ackerman wrote. After years of listening to people in my office, after years of beating on the closed doors of a church that does not listen to women, I wrote in reply,

> Listening is always a life-giving act. So many people have never been heard in their whole lives. They have raged against the deafness with alcohol and temper tantrums and sex and social paralysis but even then no one has noticed the message. We are all trying to be heard. I must listen more and better to everyone.

Most of all, I have known the value of being listened to in my own life. No set of rules, no prescriptions from on high, ever carried me through the dark or gave me courage for the heights. It was the people who took time to listen to me who gave me something more important than the rules to live by. They gave me back a sense of myself, of my own convictions, of the law of God within the heart.

"When has someone's honest and caring listening enabled you to express and transform your anger?" Jan L. Richardson wrote. And there was no doubt in my mind about that one. Over and over again I had been brought to the next step of life, of conviction, of courage, and of certainty by those who were willing to help me plumb the depths of my own heart. So I wrote,

Listeners are life's rarest breed. Parent figures, gurus, com-manders, curial overlords, and nags are easy to come by. Listeners—those who hear the pain behind the pain, allow you to probe it, and work with you to find a way beyond it—come few and far between. In all my life, I have known only two. But they have made all the difference. Thanks to them I have survived both my beginnings and my endings.

To listen to the other, to be listened to, gives us the lat-itude it takes to separate the silver from the dross both around us and in us. Orders bind us to an immediate re-sponse, but listening sets us free to think things through.

I have no doubt that the cultivation of wisdom is greater than the practice of obedience. I know in my own life that listening has always been more developmental of people than giving them orders. I am convinced that coming to un-derstand our own motives, our own principles, is more de-termining of our own spiritual life than compliance with the will of someone else will ever be. The consequences of each determine the complexion of the world around us. Most of all, they reveal us to ourselves. Jean Houston wrote once, "Our greatest genius may be the ability to prime the healing and evolutionary circuits of one another." I thought about the strange-sounding language there and decided that, yes, we do contribute to the ongoing evolution of the world, we do heal the body as much by healing the soul as by anything physical we ever do. It is an awesome insight. I wrote,

> I think Houston means that every contact is an invitation, a potential for growth. We bring something out in one an-other. We set up reactions in one another. We prod the other to new levels of thought and action. Point: Choose your friends carefully—and do not dismiss your enemies. They are creating you, too.

RESISTANCE:
THE GOSPEL IMPERATIVE

Between invocation and benediction is the possibility of speaking justice.

—Maren C. Tirabassi

Between life and death it is for all of us to do one blazing act of good—however small it may seem at the time. Life is the opportunity to speak one great truth in the face of one great lie. It may seem that no one hears it. It may seem that nothing changes. But not to speak—that is the real sin. Then, smallness is the lot even of the great. Only the doing of justice is a good enough excuse to be born.

—Joan Chittister, Journal, January 23

THE SPIRITUAL LIFE CAN BE ONE HUGE TRAP, ONE LONG excursion into unreality. The delusion of perfect peace haunts us, and we feed it on prayer and ritual and a contemplation designed to remove us from the stress and strains of the world around us. We don't pray in order to have the strength to deal with life as it is. We pray in order to ignore life as it is. We do everything we can to deny the grubby, dirty, downright frustrating character of the gospel life—no smelly lepers, no dirty cripples, no cloying blind people—for us. We want "the spiritual life," we tell ourselves. And we do it in the name of God.

During the early days of my own religious formation, I struggled to reconcile the two great spiritual opposites in my own life. We were the order that, historians said, "saved Western civilization." Well, maybe, I thought, but if so I couldn't figure out how. We called ourselves "semicloistered." People could come to visit us, but we seldom if ever went to visit them. How we were supposed to be saving civilization, I did not know. We lived behind walls, we never left the monastery grounds without permission, we needed the consent of a superior to talk to seculars in our own house, and we seldom, if ever, walked the streets. On one of those rare occasions, I and my companion—the sister assigned to go with me to a doctor's appointment—found ourselves in the middle of town on the hottest day in July. The sun was an unmerciful enemy. The heavy serge habit was wet against my back, the cotton hose and hot metal brace were rubbing my legs sore. The linen coif around my head wilted and went limp on my neck. The stern black oxfords felt heavy, and every step was an effort. Suddenly, out of nowhere, three laughing girls in shorts, halters, and sandals passed us on the street, looked back at us in that mocking way adolescents have, and laughed again. "Because they look like that," my companion said, "we look like this."

The lesson stuck with me down through the years. What exactly were we doing? What was the purpose of living in one century in the midst of another? What was there about being "strange" that was of the essence of the spiritual life? Why is reaction the only answer to social change?

The questions belie the kind of spirituality that gets out of touch with reality and so calls itself more spiritual because of it. We create a false dilemma and call it holiness: the sacred versus the secular; God versus the world; spirituality versus worldliness. We look for Jesus in the temple, but never with the crowds.

Manuals of spiritual direction from seventeenth-century France outlined steps to holiness designed to take spirituality beyond daily life to the level of the otherworldly. It structured the spiritual life on three separate levels of commitment. According to Benet of Canfield, the lowest level involved itself in the events of the world.[6] The next level struggled for interior illumination. The most spiritually advanced of all suffered the "annihilation of the self," made one simply wafted up into direct contemplation of God. For them, life on earth became a ripening time for the soul, not a time for the bringing of the reign of God. Life on earth was simply a waiting ground for heaven.

At its extreme, quietism, a distancing of the self from the things of the world in favor of heavenly things, was denounced by the church. And good thing, too, if the holiness of Jesus of Nazareth is meant to be any kind of model to the rest of us. But the ecclesiastical denunciations of quietist piety were always too brutal to be effective. Those committed to quietism only became more committed, and enemies of the Inquisition for other reasons, in sympathy with the quietists, only tolerated these ideas of the total spiritualization of the spiritual all the more. In the end, the quietist strain of spirituality left its mark on us all. Piety, rather than the prophetic tradition, remained the hallmark of the Christian for centuries to come, even in our own time.

Yet today prophets of pietism tell us to "pray for peace" and "pray that God's will be done." And that is certainly important. But they do not demand that we ourselves do something to ensure either. Instead, the professional pietist in us acts as if the Book of Genesis, with its emphasis on personal responsibility, had never been written. We fool ourselves into believing that we are supposed to live in this world as if we were living in the next. We create a devil's den of complacency and call it the spiritual life. We make quietism the ideal of the age.

Every era manufactures a heresy proper to the times. Quietism is ours. We call it "separation of church and state" now, but the effects are basically the same. Rather than defend the original meaning of the proposition that no single religion shall be our state religion, we misuse the concept to silence ourselves in the name of spirituality. We ignore the public arena and call ourselves "spiritual" for doing so. We silence ourselves in the name of spirituality. We remove ourselves from things that are "passing." We aspire to "higher things" than civil justice or care for the oppressed. We forgive ourselves our disinterest in the questions of our age on the grounds that those things have nothing to do with being Christian. Only the laws and the customs have something to do with being Christian, we argue, not the gospel.

"Pray, therefore, to the Sovereign of the harvest to send out laborers into the fields," my journal quoted from Matthew 9:38. It is an important verse. A troubling one. Ever since the Vietnam War, I have struggled between two tensions in life: to be good or to be just, to be a compliant citizen or to be a conscientious one. The journal opened the issue again. I wrote,

> It is not my responsibility to save the world, to stop the war, to change the church, to liberate women. God will see to all of that because planetary destruction, government-sponsored slaughter—for which "war" is a pornographic euphemism—ecclesiastical imperialism, and sexism are all insidious worms inside otherwise great ideas. But it is my responsibility to do something to eradicate each of them from where I stand or bear the sin of being part of all of them. Consciousness commits. Once I see that what calls itself virtue is really sin, I have no choice but to resist it. But, the end of it all depends on society's being able to achieve a critical mass of resistance. For that, God will need to "send out laborers into the field."

If there is a major problem in spirituality today, it may be that we do not do enough to form Christians for resistance to evil. We form them for patient endurance and for civil conformity. We form them to be "good" but not necessarily to be "holy." In the doing of it, we make compliant Christians rather than courageous ones, as if bearing evil were more important than confronting it. We go on separating life into parts, one spiritual, one not.

This tension between what is profane and what is spiritual makes all the difference between a holy life and a pious life. The pious life seeks spiritual consolation, a kind of otherworldly disinterest in the secular city. The holy life, if Jesus is any model at all, understands that one without the other is bogus. To be holy on earth we must pursue spiritual fulfillment in the midst of the sacred secular. This awareness of the prophetic power of the spiritual brought me face-to-face with the need to come to grips with a spirituality of resistance. It is, I decided, the relationship between power and justice that makes all the difference between seeking the kingdom of God and seeking spiritual self-satisfaction.

JUSTICE:
PASSION FOR THE REIGN OF GOD

Where there is no effort to create justice, there is no love.

—Carter Heyward

Religion is such a conundrum. We learn love there and turn it into piety rather than justice. Going to church is "religious"; "doing justice" is political! Maybe that's the point: Maybe the really religious person must, in the end, give up religion and cling to spirituality— to the essence—instead.

—Joan Chittister, Journal, August 4

I GREW UP SURROUNDED BY STATUES AND HOLY PICTURES— framed likenesses of angels and saints and Jesus and Mary. They were often plastic, usually garish, always exaggerated. But they said everything there was to say about what, at that time, I thought religion was all about.

The pictures hung on my bedroom wall; the statues sat on my dresser. We got them in school for doing perfect spelling papers or having perfect attendance or just about anything else somebody wanted us to be perfect about. These memories of other times, these idylls of the heavenly, the unearthly, the next world marked the frontiers of the spiritual world for me. They were a call to elsewhere.

Later, better versions of them—framed in gold or carved out of wood—were everywhere in the monastery, too. But whatever era they came from or whatever art form they came in, they were part of the Catholic psyche. They were the Catholic psyche.

The problem came for me when I discovered that, without any intention of my own, I had become one of them. Women religious, like the icons around them, were also pious statues in the public mind. We were the collector's items of the tradition, neuter gender and anonymous. People made nun dolls and sold them at craft fairs the same way they made teddy bears and plastic rosaries. We were the statuettes of the living tradition. But I never knew it until we began to realize that heaven wasn't just out there. Heaven started here, the reign of God started here, we came to realize. And we were to have something to do with bringing it. So, we began to live accordingly.

As George W. Bush threatened to launch a second war with Iraq, I wrote a small publication called "The Unjust War." It was in response to the long-defined Just War Theory that had been coined by Augustine in the fifth century, updated by Thomas Aquinas, preached by the Cistercians in the thirteenth century, and embedded in their 1985 document on nuclear weapons by the bishops of the United States. I had been speaking on the characteristics of a just war as laid out in this ancient theory for more than twenty years.

This new article marked my first published attempt to determine whether war could ever be just in this technological world and under these conditions. I wasn't being radical, in other words. If anything, the article was conservative, steeped in texts long considered part of the tradition and sincere in its effort to determine the place of war, if any, in modern society. Furthermore, it was a purely speculative reflection, not a call to arms, not a critique of any specific policies or plans of the U.S. government itself. But some people began to howl. They weren't upset simply because they disagreed with the material. They didn't even advert to the material. No, they were upset because, they said, I was supposed to be in a monastery and "not in politics." It was an argument that had been used against me, against my whole community, ever since the emergence of peace demonstrations during the Vietnam War. I had answered that question for myself a long time ago. Now the journal triggered it in me again: "Unless we are involved in naming the evil in the world, we could slip into the silence of racism, sexism and ageism," Elizabeth Francis Caldwell wrote. And I agreed, not out of any particular political bias, but because I had seen Jesus do it over and over again with the Pharisees. I wrote,

> The truth is, I think, that what we don't name we enable. We become blind to the evils in which we live and breathe and call our culture. We take the unacceptable as natural. We take injustice for granted. We call sin normal. But if and when we begin to call evil, evil . . . then we ourselves begin to confront the problem.

The concept seems clear enough when the protest is a public one. Public protest is part and parcel of being American. But there is a two-edged sword embedded in the principle of protest. If and when the evil—the clear and intentional harm of one by another—is more private than public, then, somehow or other, the justification of dissent begins to waver. The more difficult decision comes when the passion for justice conflicts with the practices of the church itself. Then, what does spirituality demand: obedience—conformity to the system—or obedience—to the spirit of the gospel?

It's questions like these that test what religion is about against what religion itself is meant to be. It is a question women live with every day of their lives. If we believe that religion gives us a mirror into the mind of God, but the mind of God and the mind of the system are at odds, the tension can be overwhelming. Some women leave the church because for them it would be irreligious to stay. Other women stay in the system because the most religious part of them demands that religion itself be called to its best. The journal touched the problem in me over and over again. "The only way we can move ahead is by living the reality we envision," Ada-Maria Isasi-Diaz wrote. I have seen the cost of that for women, and I wrote back out of my own struggle to stay faithful to the church and committed to the gospel at the same time:

> Unless we begin to be the church we want, that church will never come. And yet, those who do it—and are discovered—will be ground to dust by that very church. It is a hard bargain: shall we die for this church as it must be or at the hands of this church as it is. I for one must simply go on—and let the seeds bloom where they can, the chips fall where they may, and life take whatever turn for better or worse that befalls me.

The conflict comes when we begin to realize that justice is a conscience question of its own. Those who love a system enough to want it to be what it says it is, too often find themselves labeled the enemy within. What is moral here; where does justice lie: to call the church itself to grow—and so run the risk of undermining its credibility, or to excuse the sins of the church and so run the risk of dooming it to condemnation by the very gospel it claims to preach? The journal raised the issue clearly: "Whom do I close myself against?" Deena Metzger wrote. The question is a piercing one. It is so easy to become hardened against any system that has become hardened against you. I have known the struggle it takes to be a loyal part of a dysfunctional family for a long, long time. I wrote,

> I don't think I "close myself" against anyone. But I do know that I have made up my mind never to give myself away again to anyone or anything that simply wants to use me for its own interests or against my own. I spent my life supporting a church that wants nothing to do with women— and by staying in it, even to protest it, may be doing it yet . . . I am plagued by dishonesty. Am I really saying what I believe? Am I really doing what I want to do? Am I simply "putting a good face on an inherently bad thing"? And if so, I am part of the problem in the church. I and my kind hold it up, give it a legitimacy its illegitimacy does not deserve. As long as the church rejects women, it is no church at all.

The soul struggles in these in-between times with feelings of frustration, feelings of infidelity. Is the problem in the system—or in the self? Are we too bold—or not brave enough? Does virtue lie in endurance—or in indignation? Is it better to wait for time to change things—or can time possibly change anything if the change doesn't first start in us? Through us? Georgia O'Keeffe wrote, "I decided to start anew . . . to accept as true my own thinking. This was one of the best times of my life." That's fine for a woman who lives unattached to an institution, who is the center and the

fulcrum of her own life. But what about the rest of us who
live in systems like marriage and religious life that demand
conformity in return for security, that rest on public norms
and traditional roles, good—even understandable as these
may be—in many cases? What about those who live alone
and are neither wealthy enough or talented enough not to
have to compromise with any system to survive—the government, the corporation, the subsistence systems of life
that regularly discard truth tellers of any ilk? I wrote,

> Well, it may work for Georgia O'Keeffe but it's a long, hard
> journey for anyone else. To begin to believe your own truth
> is to begin to withdraw from dogmatism, institutionalism,
> authoritarianism, and parentalism. These things conspire to
> keep a woman "nice." They also manage to keep a person
> under control and underdeveloped. But I think my own
> truth anyway—as God has enabled me.

Thinking our own truth and claiming that truth are two
different things, however. Lots of people think lots of
things—but they don't say them. They know that saying them
out loud would change their lives. They know they would have
to make changes in their own lives and perhaps even threaten
the lives of those around them. They know that claiming their
own truth is the first step off the edge of a mountain alone.
It's not strange that so many people keep so silent.

What is strange is that we are not more outspoken together. If it is because we don't want to hurt anything, we
may well be missing the messages of history. The spirituality of silence kills, too—both ourselves and others. Ask the
churches in World War II Germany if that's not so. They
preached religion, but what spirituality did they practice: the
spirituality of Jesus before Pilate, who questioned his ques-

tioners and contended against evil to the end, or the spirituality of Peter with the maidservant, who shrank from public
proclamation of his Christian commitment? We proclaim
Jesus, but we really follow Peter. And we do it all in order to
do good, in order not to do more harm, in order to keep the
peace. "God gives us the strength and courage to resist injustice and to transform suffering," Marie M. Fortune wrote.
But that's easier to say than it is to believe. I wrote,

> But does God give us the strength and courage to pay the
> price for resisting injustice and transforming suffering? I
> just finished writing *The Story of Ruth: Twelve Moments in Every
> Woman's Life*. Some women readers find it "too prophetic."
> They fear to be thought of as "harsh and negative"—not
> soft enough, not "spiritual" enough. Talk about racism or
> militarism and they're fine. But talk to them about the op-
> pression of women and they're afraid of hurting men. . . . I
> think that is the real lesson of this period: If you want to
> be treated as a full human being, an adult, a peer, you must
> claim it for yourself and let them all deal with it later.

The love of justice spreads danger everywhere it goes.
It is dangerous to the old order and dangerous to the self as
well. Those who speak up, speak first, speak loudly, almost
always speak alone. We let them do it for the rest of us. So
Bonhoeffer dies, Gandhi dies, King dies, Kennedy dies. We
trample down the spirits of those whose bodies we leave in-
tact and run them off the grounds. Curran goes, Grammick
goes, Willigus Jaeger goes. And the whole body dies a little
bit more every day. What is important, it seems to me, is
that we do not allow the spirit to die in us at the same time.

Mary Catherine Bateson said, "Each of us constructs a
life that is her own central metaphor for thinking about the

world." I wrote back what I knew to be at the heart of my own life and the lives of many around me:

> My metaphor for thinking about the world is "The Beloved of God." It means that I must tie my life to the voice of God in my heart as I hear it through the poor, the oppressed, the disenfranchised, and those with voices other than the voice of the institutions. For that I may be rejected by the system, of course, but I cannot keep my soul and do otherwise.

Chapter Seventeen

POWER IN THE POWERLESS: THE COURAGE TO REFUSE EVIL

Just when we perceive ourselves as powerful, when we believe in that power, we appropriate the power within us.

—Barbara Starrett

I do not perceive myself as "powerful." I perceive myself as strong— as able to endure, yes, but not as able to change things. And the ability to change things, to work your will, whether anyone else likes it or not, is the real essence of power. It is a tragic distinction—this contradiction between power and strength—because it unmasks the difference between the powerful and the powerless, between an oppressor and a victim. Worst of all, I am not sure whether the problem is in the environment—or in me. Maybe I am simply failing to do what I ought to do, whatever the price to be paid.

—Joan Chittister, Journal, January 4

IT HAPPENED ONLY ONCE, BUT IT AFFECTED ME FOR THE rest of my life. In 1976, the Vatican issued its first explanation for the nonordination of women. Why, women asked, could good, committed, spiritual, baptized women not also be priests? Because, Rome said, women didn't look like men. End of discussion. End of theological development. End of consistency of the faith. But it was also the beginning of an entirely new flood of questions. As in, Is the Eucharist an event of the Christian community or simply an historical drama we are replaying? Do we celebrate Eucharist "in remembrance of Him" or "in imitation of Him?" Did Jesus "become flesh," as in fully human, or did Jesus simply become male, as in a particular gender and for the sake of that gender?

It isn't that I hadn't struggled with those questions for years. In fact, I burned inside at the high-handedness of such a nonresponse to such serious theological concerns. Most of all, as then president of the largest group of women religious in the world, I was empowered—expected, in fact—to speak on their behalf for the concerns of women everywhere. But I didn't. Not really. I spoke, of course. But in a way that completely ignored the inconsistency of the answer. Instead, my official response was short and bland; oh, very true, yes, but very, very political. The statement I put out said, "Now that we understand what the issue is we can study it." It was the perfect answer of the perfect victim in the face of perfect power. It was "nice." It wasn't "aggressive." It did everything but whimper. And it did nothing at all to advance the question of the role of women in the church or to invite dialogue.

The consternation on the faces of the women who came to talk to me about the public statement said it all. For political reasons, I explained—in the hope of being able to pursue the question and at the same time not to split the conference over an issue that was not only not yet vital to every member, but even confusing to many—I had said nothing. I had opted to save the organization rather than to "speak truth to power." And in that act, truth as I knew it in the depths of me wasted away.

I knew then and there that I would never do that again. I would never again squander the tiny space a woman has to say anything of value. I had played at mock peacemaking where there was no peace. I had failed to claim my own power and in that failure failed to empower others, as well.

Power is a frightening thing. In a society of educated adults who are quite capable of thinking things through for themselves, of coming to grips with them as a group, of dealing with the implications of them in their own personal lives, it is also a travesty. Only sheep need to be driven. People need to be led.

Now years later, the journal challenged me again on the nature and place of power: "For the sake of power, it is often necessary to set the world upside down," Deena Metzger wrote. Of course it is. If you can. But there is another side to the issue, as well. Every woman, every minority, every child knows it. It is the issue of the powerless. I wrote,

> The concept of power is based precisely on being able to turn another person's world upside down. It is the ability to do our own will whatever its effect on the other. That is why power is so often destructive: our own will and the means to enforce it blot out the rest of the world. We become the god of our small universe. It is a paltry heaven to have. . . .

This is power "over" others. This is the power that turns a people into pawns and serfdom into slavery. This is the power of those people and institutions and nations that are too big, too strong, too overwhelming, too well defended to be opposed, too politically placed to be bridled.

The United States of America went to war with Iraq precisely because it had such power. And only because it had such power. If there had been another nation strong enough to challenge our wealth and our military technology, we would have negotiated the issues, not invaded the country. We did not, for instance, invade the Soviet Union or China. We waited for over forty years for the tensions to settle. We didn't even invade North Korea, a country that was doing the very things we said the Iraqis were—and at the very same time. We negotiated with North Korea because North Korea had the strength to oppose us, and we knew it. We continued to send diplomats to discuss the issues for years and years.

Power is a factor in ecclesiastical matters, as well as political ones. Theology is what it is only because centralized churches have such power. If the poor, the women, and the dispossessed sat at the tables where theological decisions are made, there would be a different set of sins.

So where does balance lie? We need authority, of course, and authority—to have authority—needs power. We all belong to something bigger than we are. It's in the nature of that belonging that we stand to lose the part of ourselves that must never be given away. The only thing we have that is peculiar to us—our own truth, our own special experience of life—stands to be lost, if not suppressed, in the interest of an organization that exists for its own aggrandizement rather than for the development of its members. Then our own insights become lost to the accumulation of human wisdom. To be truly and totally human, to be accountable for our own humanity, we must struggle with the question of balance to the end. "For this is our God and we are the people of God's pasture and the sheep of God's hand," Psalm 95 says. I wrote in response:

> It is sometimes very difficult to know where God is for us: in the demands of authority for obedience to the sins they call virtue—for the nonordination of women, for instance—in the name of "unity." Or is God in the questions of the heart

that deserve to be pursued—that demand to be answered—
in the light of the rest of the gospel. And so the question
haunts me: Would Jesus stay in the church today? In any of
them? And, if not, who would follow him out of it? Would
I? Yes, there's the question. I have lived a lifetime of ecclesiastical sins: no "mixed marriages," they taught, and then
changed their minds; no burial for fetuses; no moral absolutes about wife beating; no protection of Jews; no resistance to segregation. And I went along with all of them.

So which sin is greater? Theirs or mine?

The major question, the nagging question, the question
conscience wails at us in an era of holocausts and genocide
and "collateral damage" and the unmitigated power of
global corporations, pales all the rest of them. It is, And
what can I possibly do about it? I have no power with which
to challenge this power. I have no connections to wheedle
and deal. I have no inside track by which to work my will
even through another. For the Christian, the problem carries
with it the very essence of integrity. How can one be a
Christian and not do anything about these things? "Do not
be conformed to this world but be transformed by the renewal of your mind," Paul wrote in Romans 12. Ever since
that day in 1976, Vietnam on one side and the woman's issue on the other, I wrestled with the implications of it.
What kind of insanity must it be to confront that which we
have not a hope of besting? And on the other hand, what
kind of sanity can we possibly claim if we don't? Finally, in
response to the Letter of Paul to the Romans, I wrote,

> Exactly how does a person go about not being "conformed to
> this world"? We live in the belly of the beast. It is our politi-
> cians, our banks, our businesses that cheat poor laborers,
> make the dirty military alliances, sell the weapons, hike up the

interest rates. And we are the ones who buy from them, and elect them, and collect their dividends. Is there any hope for our own purity of soul in such a world as this? Is there any hope for mine? Well, Paul seems to think so. He says, "Be transformed by the renewal of your mind." Change the way you think, in other words. And say so. That's what I must do. Whatever the ridicule, whatever the criticism, I must say so. Loudly, clearly, always. Then maybe someday I will find myself lost in a chorus of voices all shouting "no" together. And then the world will change.

Intractable as the powers that surround us are, somewhere along the way I had discovered the spirituality of powerlessness. This is power "for."

In the end power does not lie in wealth and authority; it lies in having nothing to lose. When we have nothing to lose or to gain in a situation, we are finally free. Then, the only things that stand between us and integrity are consciousness and truth. Powerlessness does not neutralize us; it drives us on. We are the only ones on the battlefields of life with an eye on the questions alone. Everybody else is too busy calculating the effect of the loss of the situation on their reputations and their careers and their images and their positions. The powerless go naked into combat and cannot be scarred. They alone have the power to endure it all.

"By refusing to endure evil and by seeking to transform suffering, we are about God's work of making justice and healing brokenness," Marie M. Fortune wrote. By this time, I knew the contradictions between power and powerlessness. I wrote,

> I love the concept of "refusing to endure evil." It does not imply that we will best it, simply that we will refuse to endure it. It makes refusal the virtue for which we get no training. We

are trained to "obey," which means to accept, to condone, to participate in it, to comply. "I refuse"—though in the end it may change nothing—is still the power not to agree. "I refuse." Those are strong words, holy words. "I refuse."

Language—words—is the love of my life. I see in words the seed of every possibility, the resistance to every evil. It is only when we speak that there is any hope of change. But once we realize that, then we realize that the real spiritual question is not, Do I have the power to change this? The real spiritual question is, Do I have the courage to say no to it?

FEMINIST SPIRITUALITY: THE COMING OF A NEW WORLD

Our society's hope and our planet's survival lie in our capacity to free ourselves from rigid gender roles.

—Rita Nakashima Brock

Until we can all be fully human together—until we can all come into the wholeness of ourselves, neither men nor women will be really happy. Men will go on being threatened, women will go on being half developed. What kind of world is that? I was not born to wash a man's socks. He was not born to make my decisions. I want no part of such slavery, not even when you couch it in God-talk.

—Joan Chittister, Journal, March 18

IN AFGHANISTAN THEY HAVE BEGUN TO ALLOW GIRLS TO GO to school. In India they have instituted legislation against bride burnings. In Ethiopia, African women and the First Ladies of Burkina Faso, Nigeria, Mali, and Guinea gathered to condemn and protest the practice of the genital mutilation of young girls that is practiced in twenty-eight countries in Africa and the Middle East. In the United States of America, women are struggling for welfare support for single mothers, for day care programs for the children of single parents, for wage equity, and for as much financial support for women's sports as for men's. Everywhere women are seeking a voice in public affairs.

In the meantime, men everywhere are threatening wholesale slaughter in the name of defense. Violence on the scale it is practiced now and here and by us—two hundred fifty wars in the twentieth century alone, most of them with a religious component—is clearly a sin against the sacrament of life. What's wrong with this picture? What's wrong with us? We stand on the brink of human extinction boasting that we seek the God of life. We invoke religion as a justification for oppressing other religions. What clearer proof do we have

148

that our differences are not about religion; they are in the name of religion, but are founded on reasons that are totally irreligious. And what can women do about it, if anything?

The questions have haunted me for years. "What gifts can women offer as humankind struggles to find meaning in the present and shape a meaningful future for generations to come?" Lynne Mobberley Deming wrote. I knew the importance of the question. I had begun my forays into feminism, thinking that the whole sick, dangerous, and distorted order of things was simply a male conspiracy against women. As the years went by, I began to think differently. I began to see the issues in terms of the power and powerlessness of both men and women, as much as in terms of the differences in maleness and femaleness. I began to realize that sexism and racism and classism were of a piece, that they existed to keep the powerful in power. And I knew, too, that each of them spawned a distinct value system, a distinct way of seeing the world. I wrote in response to the Deming statement,

> I think there are all manner of things a woman can offer the world. I'm just not sure it's because we're women. It may be because we're the universal underclass. We know what it is to live a life of humility, peace, compassion, and resignation. We have learned to cope with what we did not have the power to change. Whatever it is that makes women different, this world needs it. The problem is that the qualities—the values—that women embody are not considered premium in this culture. In this culture, we don't value female servant-hood; we don't care about niceness; we don't think things through, we force them through. If anything, what a woman is or has developed is simply overlooked. Or derided.

When the newly emerging agricultural societies began to acquire land for themselves, the human worldview changed to support it. Gone were the egalitarian communities of a hunter-gathering people. Conquest, power, pride, authoritarianism, competition, and "reason" became the dominant characteristics of dominant peoples. And dominant men. Ownership, hierarchy, and control became society's hallmark. Everything—and everyone—was owned by someone strong enough to own it or them. God became male—and males became God. Or vice versa. One of Anne Carr's entries in the journal read, "Christian feminism and the spiritual vision it entails is a transforming grace for our times." And I thought to myself, that's true—but will it really ever come to pass? I wrote,

> When all the money, all the power, and all the force are on one side, it is hard to imagine what could finally transform it except the psychological needs of men themselves. What will motivate them to give up their social harems except the great gaping emptiness that must come from having to pretend forever that you are more than you are.

My mother loved mechanics and construction and challenge—everything a woman was supposed to consider unfeminine. What's worse, she was good at them. "Dutch," she'd say to my father, "we don't have to hire someone to tile that bathroom. We can do it ourselves." But he couldn't. And he had no intention of letting her tell him how. So she cut and measured and leveled the tile herself, and he sulked for days. On the other hand, he had a way with children she admired, but never understood. He could play monopoly on the floor with giggling eight-year-olds and love it. The nieces and nephews followed him around like the Pied Piper while he made up things for us to do. Her idea of a good child was one that played alone somewhere else. Both of them, I came to realize as the years went by, were being strangled in a system that told them what they were supposed to do in order to be what the system said they were—and they weren't.

But the other side of the person and the other side of the system never came to light, never came to be valued. Feeling, compassion, humility, dialogue, nonviolence all became the virtues of the weak. But, ironically, it is the strong who need them most.

Feminist spirituality is a whole new worldview. If we are to save this world, we need to cultivate it now, not because it is "female"—which, given the number of male feminists there are, is obviously not true—but because it is humane. Because it is truly human. Because without it, the very globe is in danger. "Feminism is an all-encompassing perspective on the whole of reality," Janet Kalven and Mary I. Buckley said. And I know the truth of it because it has changed my whole life, the way I see the world, and even the way I see Jesus and religion. I wrote in response,

> Indeed feminism changes the way we see everything, not just the way we relate to men. It changes what we value and what we seek. It changes the way we see ourselves as women. And it turns a critical—and calloused—eye on both state and church. After that there is no going back to "ladylike" docility or clerical worship. After that there is only God and me.

The worldview we have inherited in a mechanical, technological world of superpowers and underdeveloped peoples thrives on reason—that quality of thought that eliminates feeling as a basis for action—and its unreasonable assumption that women and children are simply "collateral damage" in the male pursuit of preeminence. Reason in this world functions on the cold, calculating notion that might makes right and that feelings are a sign of failure. But only feelings, not reason, carry the label "humanity guaranteed." Feelings enable us to remember pain so that we dare not inflict it. Feelings require us to spend ourselves on love so we do not betray it. Feelings give us a vision for the beautiful in a world bent on the ugly victimization of whole peoples. Feelings are the hallmark of a feminist spirituality. Sheryl Nicholson's entry in the journal said, "Gifts of the heart are what memories are made of." I have a feeling that memory is one of the first casualties of a canny, calculating patriarchal world. I wrote,

> I have a theory that only what touches the heart is really lodged in the mind. Memory is made up of what has touched our lives. So, in later years, the data drops away because it is useless. But soft touches, hard words, deep joys, great pain never leave us. For good or ill, they remain. They are always there, soothing us or torturing our souls. The life question it leaves us with may be worth thinking about, What do we do with the feelings that clog our souls?

It is time, I think, to release feeling into the world.

It is time to give feminist values their place so that women and men can both be whole human beings. It is time to give women—the other half of the human race, the other face of God—a place in the salvation of both our religions and our nations. It is time to allow men the right to be soft of heart, humble, compassionate, and unafraid to be vulnerable. It is time for women, the life bearers, to bring to the world the feminist spirituality this present world lacks. It is time for women to assume as much responsibility for maintaining the life of the world as they do for bearing the life of the world. Otherwise, women simply birth one patriarchal world to destroy the other.

Feminist spirituality has as much to do with being a holy man as it does with being a mature woman. It does not divide women from men. On the contrary, it simply closes the gap between the powerful and the powerless, so that both women and men can have fullness of life—a feeling for it as well as a reason for manipulating it—"and have it more abundantly."

Chapter Eighteen

SOCIETY AND WOMEN: THE LOSS OF SOUL

In the past ten or fifteen years women have begun to trust each other.

—Elizabeth Strahan

The world of women has finally become a world of wisdom, strength, and support. We have counted our value for so long in terms of our relationship to men that we have missed the meaning of a woman's life. Only now are we able to prefer our own tastes, our own insights, our own company. It is a time of deep, deep revelation of the self through the mirror that is the other.

—Joan Chittister, Journal, March 13

WHEN GALILEO STOOD UP, TELESCOPE IN HAND, TO argue that the sun did not revolve around the Earth, but that the Earth revolved around the sun, the very foundations of theology shifted. Man, the church argued, was God's highest creature and therefore had to be the center of the universe. In 1633, they tried Galileo for heresy in a church court, found him guilty, and sentenced him to house arrest for life. But truth has a way of persisting. Medieval clerics lost that round, and rounds to come, to science. Science made it more and more clear every day: "man" was not the center of the universe. And science went its own way.

But there is very little proof that either the church or patriarchal society at large ever really changed their minds about the notion that men, the male of the species, were meant to rule. Certainly not science itself; clearly not the government; definitely not the church. And so, not only science went its own way. Women began to go their own way, too.

The spiritual fallout of the loss of the woman's agenda in the public arena is incalculable. Governments attend to male agendas and make decisions according to male perspectives and male value systems. The church inherited a male God and all the implications that go with it for marriage law, social hierarchies, sacramental systems, and ecclesiastical pomp and power. Science, on the other hand, found just what it set out to look for in its tests: women were weak of body and of mind, too emotional to lead, too limited to learn. They needed a man "to be their head." They were fit only to be mothers and, ironically, unfit even for that as male doctors took over the birthing process and male social scientists devolped child-rearing theories from academic towers where women were seldom permitted.

As a result, the major social systems of the world have been working with only half the resources of the human race. Theology and ministry have lost the wisdom of the feminine. So much for Mary of Nazareth and the God who is "pure spirit," neither male nor female, but the essence of both.

The effect on society of this great gaping loss is immeasurable. The disconnect lights up on TV screens everywhere: burkas in the Middle East, sex slaves in the Far East, machismo in South America, illiteracy in Africa, political invisibility in the West, and economic inferiority everywhere. Women are ornamental, not valuable.

But there is a new spirit rising that challenges every structure on earth, even the white male God. The journal included a quotation from Connie Zweig. "Feminism created sisterhood," Zweig wrote, "a realignment of women with women." I had experienced it myself in 1974. As priests processed down the center of the hotel ballroom, all vested to say Mass for a national gathering of women religious, a new consciousness cried out loud to be heard. While the priests sang the opening hymn, the women around me were singing, too. But the women were changing the pronouns in the opening hymn of the liturgy from "him" to "them" as they sang. "I will raise him up," the priests sang. "I will raise 'them' up," the women sang even louder. Little by little, the chorus grew from five women to twenty-five to fifty to two hundred fifty women. And finally, the revolution spread to the whole ballroom. And to me. For the first time in my life, I knew not only that the system was wrong, but that I was not the only one who knew it. It was a moment of genuine rebirth. I wrote in the journal in response to Zweig,

> I could not live without the sensitivity of women—as much as I enjoy the company of men. I feel in the presence of men, however, like a traveler in a foreign land. They dismiss or minimize what I consider important. They exaggerate what I consider trivial. They seek the approval only of other men, most of whose standards are white, male, Western, and Roman—with everything those categories imply and most of which I reject as superficial and sexist.

The spiritual implications for a society that cuts the feminine out of the center of its political and theological arenas take on a proportion too long ignored.

We have become single-minded. We see things only through the male eye. We know God only through the male mind. We recognize the spirit only in the male model. As a result, we can go to war, and no one at the table will talk about the effect of carpet bombing on the eardrums of babies. We can pass church laws that cut women off from discernment about the very things that we say affect their eternal souls. We can argue in favor of the so-called just war that we know will kill thousands, but condemn birth control outright simply because it averts birth. We can use women to supply the support structure for a society that devalues what women do, but rely on it in order to free men to make money. We live with shriveled souls.

Things are changing, of course. The role of women is at least a question now. But what kind of world do we live in, how holy are we really, when the intellectual and spiritual status of half the human race is a question at all? And what is the answer to that? Barbara Starrett's entry in the journal makes it seem easy. She writes, "Every woman's efforts are valuable and limited only by her own vision and the intensity of her belief in that vision." But I read it remembering the pain in the eyes of Turkish women as they talked about the lack of civil rights for women.

I read it thinking of Marta, the unmarried "wife" of a man in Mexico who, like the rest of the culture, takes two "wives" for granted and supports neither one of them completely. And all the while, social standards there make a man and children imperative for the "good" woman and the single woman suspect.

I read it thinking of Gloria, the abandoned welfare woman on our block whose aid had been cut, but who couldn't afford child care for the children left at home while she worked. So they labeled the children "deprived" and called her a bad mother.

I read it knowing too many middle-class women whose salaries are necessary now to meet family expenses, but who get no help with the housework because housework is still woman's work in the minds of men who consider themselves above it.

So I wrote that night,

> Starrett is correct, of course, but it is not a lesson easily learned. When every signal in society—the titles, the money, the positions, the uniforms, the tasks—all tell a woman she is second, not equal, not wanted, it is not easy to think, even to yourself, that what you do is really valuable. I remember as a child being ashamed of the fact that I was "only a girl." Now I am ashamed that I don't do more for other women, not simply for our sake but for the sake of the world itself—both its women and its men.

Perhaps the most serious spiritual implication of all this lies in the fact that we are now at the point that we risk wallowing in self-deception. Only in the last half of the twentieth century did women begin to break down educational barriers and enter new social arenas. Only then did women historians begin to uncover the unpublished, unhung, unmarketed works of women from centuries past. Only then did the brave ones begin to write about the kind of harems the West had constructed for its own women: the closeted wife of the nuclear family whose role was to maintain the "conspicuous consumption"[7] that demonstrated her husband's success. Only then could ideas like these ever hope to see the light of day in print. And that's the problem.

Now we take the words for granted, but we fail to admit that nothing much has changed as a result of them. Except for a few cosmetic changes here and there, women are still paid less, promoted less, hired less, valued less than men in similar positions. Women work, but only at the lower end of every category. They run for office, but can't get the money for the big campaigns and so hold less than 10 percent of the seats. They earn money, but always less than a man makes for the same kind of work. They write high theological treatises, but are never permitted to preach. And professors who claim to support equality still teach whole college courses in philosophy, theology, science, and the arts without so much as a mention of the women who are also central to their fields. That's what's wrong with the kind of equality that breeds inequity.

We are deceiving ourselves. General semanticists tell us that one of the most common pitfalls of language is to make the words, the promises, the proclamations, the thing. We call ourselves a "free country," for instance, and in the saying of it assume we are. So we never think that what we hear from the media might be being controlled or censored or distorted by various interest groups—and not "free" in the fullest sense at all. We make the word the thing.

In the same way, too, as long as people change pronouns—or talk about equality—we assume we have it. We risk the worst of spiritual evils—self-deception. And in most part, it is the churches that give moral substance to the sin, telling us that God made us equal—but different.

Yet, at the same time, I go on living with the memory of that ballroom and all those women changing the sexist words of the hymn right in the face of the system that said they must be maintained. In that ballroom, for the first time in my life, I knew not only that I was part of the powerless, but that the powerless had power. If women worked together, women, however apparently powerless, could change the unchangeable. And we must.

Chapter Nineteen

MEN AND WOMEN:
THE DISCOVERY OF THE ADULT

*That which is born of the flesh is flesh, and that which is born of the
Spirit is spirit.*

—John 3:6

*What does it mean to be "born of the flesh" and "born of the spirit"
and in the end does it really make any difference? So much in me
"born of the flesh"—done to satisfy my appetites—has in the end
changed my spirit. And many times for the good.*

*And those things in me "born of the spirit"—meant to be ideal-
istic, "spiritual"—have just as many times been corrupting. I was
a "good Catholic" and so became disdainful of those who weren't
Catholic. How unholy can a person be? So now I suspect the separation of flesh and spirit and am open to both. That way, perhaps
someday holiness will sneak in when I'm not looking.*

—Joan Chittister, Journal, February 28

THE PLANNING MEETING WAS GOING SMOOTHLY,
whatever the sticky financial issues on the agenda. No one
doubted that the problems were real. The differences lay in
how to deal with them. Give fewer services, hire fewer staff,

take fewer invitations, raise more money? "I think part of the answer is that we should have men on this board," one woman said. "I know that people here don't agree with that. They want to keep this a woman's thing." She paused a moment. "Maybe it's a generational difference," she said, looking up and down the table at the older women there. "But couples my age don't think like that anymore. We have partnership marriages. We're perfectly equal. And I think men raise money better than women do."

The comments made the cultural divide plain. What was really in question here: female chauvinism or the spiritual imperative for both men and women to come to the point where they recognize the spiritual value to both of them in the full development of women? The spiritual challenge is not to answer the question too quickly. Both positions have spiritual advantages; both have spiritual pitfalls. Women acting alone demonstrate female competence, but can be marginalized. Women acting together with men speak to us of mutuality, but can be lost in false partnerships.

The spiritual implications of female chauvinism have cosmic significance. If feminist spirituality deteriorates into mere femaleness, and its goal becomes the control or diminishment of men now, rather than women, as it has been for several millennia, it would only be patriarchy's last late trick on the human race. It would simply be the urge to power for its own sake, this time by females rather than males. It would mean that women would have nothing but what men have now—tension, competition, conquest, determinative power, and hierarchy. Nothing would change in the world except that this time the oppressors would be women.

The spiritual meaning of the second state, the full and independent development of women as women, is just as consequential—but different. It does change the world. Ironically enough, the development of women does not destroy marriage. It is the basis for partnership marriages and real equality and the release into the public arena of the resources of the other half of the world. But this recognition of the talents and import of women in the public sphere can't happen if women are blocked from acting independently, from being seen as fully functioning adults in their own right. It can't happen if women themselves, by being pathologically passive, simperingly docile, and unthinkingly "obedient," allow it to exist. But the public visibility of independent women must increase if women everywhere are ever to be free. Women who are enslaved, abused, and invisible themselves need to see women operating singly, separately, and apart from men, as well as with them. Why? Because what we can see we know we, too, can become.

When the United Nations Conference on Women was scheduled in Beijing, people began to argue that, given the status of women in China, a women's conference should not be held there. And certainly not under the aegis of the United Nations. I took the opposite position. I felt that the low status of women in China was exactly the reason why the conference had to be held there. It was not what we would say that would change Chinese women—their government wouldn't even permit an official delegation of Chinese women to attend it. What Chinese women would see that would change things—at least eventually—would be women from all over the world walking freely down their streets, being interviewed on their television sets, holding press conferences in their hotels. That awareness alone would seed the reformation in their hearts. They would see women, just like themselves, walking free, alone, and proud. Then they would learn who they were, who they could be, without a word having been said. They would see a new world. They would learn its possibilities.

"There is another sense," Mary Catherine Bateson's journal entry said, "in which learning can be coming home." Having learned too slowly what it meant to be a woman myself, I wrote back,

> Learning—for the learner—is surely coming home to the self. Without it, we can never become everything we are meant to become. It stretches us beyond ourselves to the core of ourselves. It gives us the tools to understand ourselves. And it also puts us in the dangerous position of having questions the system cannot answer.

Learning who we are is part of being worthy of a partnership. There is also a spiritual reason for men to see women as discrete and effective public figures. It produces a sense of self-confident pride in the woman, yes, but it also requires humility of heart in the man. If a woman is a whole person, if she can do things for herself, and if a man finds himself compelled to recognize this, then she is clearly his equal. She is definitely worth having as a wife. She is, as Scripture says in Proverbs 31:10, "a valiant woman," a woman versed in the ways of the world. A partner.

But for both men and women to come to fullness, both together and alone, women must be free to develop as fully as the men around them. Their lives must also be nurtured for greatness and nourished with pride. Women's lives must be seen as more than their biology, and men's lives must not be denied development of the human heart. Across the world, we are yet light-years away from both.

Nancy J. Berneking and Pamela Carter Joern's journal entry said, "To tell our stories and speak the truth of our experience is one way to plant a garden." After a lifetime of watching bright women be overlooked and even rejected, however smoothly, because, by being bright or self-confident or creative, they were "unfeminine," I wrote,

> But if you are a woman, who wants to hear your story? The garden is called quicksand, the place you should not go, the people you should not talk to, the books you should not read, if you are going to be a "nice" woman. The planting of it is called "dissent," "heresy." But till it we must. I sometimes wonder what my own life would have been like if I had had the sense to simply keep quiet, to accept their terms. One thing for sure, I would not be on clerical blacklists right now. And just as surely, I would only be half a human being, as well.

Feminist spirituality demands that women become adults. It's that simple. They must learn to take responsibility for their ideas. They must, if they believe that the Holy Spirit works in everyone, begin to speak their truth themselves. And at whatever the cost. They have no right to hide behind men, to manipulate men, to get what they want by wheedling and whining, rather than by claiming it for themselves honestly and strongly. "Conflict is a necessity if women are to build for the future," Jean Baker Miller said. It's a potent insight. To be a woman takes strong stuff. And now stronger than ever. She must learn to make her way in the marketplace of ideas so that the human race has all the ideas available at its service. That means learning to speak as well as to listen. For men, it means learning to listen, as well as to speak. It means learning to learn from a woman. It means dealing with the spiritual impact of humility on a world gone mad with male arrogance. I wrote in response to Miller's statement,

> Conflict—meaning the ability to pursue an independent course in the face of opposition—is contrary to a woman's formation. She's trained to be "nice," to be "docile," to be "sweet." And to be those things she has to give herself away every time someone else wants something other than she does. To be a woman, then, it is necessary to learn to sail against the tide. It costs.

I have a notion that we'll know the world has become healthy—has become holy—when we no longer think in terms of either women or men. The world—science, religion, politics—has stereotyped women for so long that it has ceased to see either women or men as real individuals. Behavioral scientists, using participant feedback, came up with a list of adjectives to describe men and women that showed us how really sick we had become. Everything said of men was positive—"brave," "active," "strong." Everything said of women was neurotic, passive, or weak—"emotional," "passive," "fearful."[8] But the truth is that some men do not like contact sports; some women do. Some men love to cook; some women don't. Some men want the opportunity to lead; some women do, too. Sexism stamps out differences and gives us stereotypes instead.

In a world of role definitions and a theology of gender, sexual stereotypes are built right into the spiritual life. The whole idea that God will work through some facets of creation, but not through others, defies the whole definition of God. Even more than that, it ignores the science of difference. Difference is the very dynamic of creation. It is difference that makes life possible, that gives life variety, that demonstrates the glory of God in all its facets. But instead of seeing differences as a sign of the limitlessness of God's presence and God's power, we have allowed them to be confined and controlled. "Women differ among themselves," Ann Belford Ulanov wrote. "We must make room for the differences." The idea is right, I'm convinced, but the problem remains. I wrote back,

> Difference is not yet a thing we prize. Conformity is the unspoken, the hidden, the insidious goal. So we shape people into systems, pour them into molds, teach them by unspoken means to keep unspoken laws. Then we wonder why it is that cultures, communities, churches die. There is no room for the newness of the Spirit in them. And they call it "tradition."

Clearly, our degree of commitment to the emergence of feminist spirituality marks the quality of our spiritual lives. We can go on forming people in the molds that make a patriarchal system run or we can let loose the Holy Spirit to sweep dangerously through the world. We can commit ourselves to bringing out the strengths in ourselves by admitting the weaknesses in us, in men as well as women, until we are all a creation in full concert with the creator. The suppression of women is a sin, not because it is a sin against women, but because it is a sin against creation itself. To suppress half of God's creation in the name of God is a sin against the Holy Spirit for which we have no name.

Change—conversion—calls us to a new sense of each other and of the self. When women are valued as fully as men, men will gain the right to be weak, to be real, to be truthful with themselves and others. Women will gain the right to learn from failure, to try again, to be co-creators with the God who made them, too, in "God's own image." Neither men nor women will be weakened by it. We will, on the contrary, be doubly strengthened. "Change is the manifestation of our ability to grow and become," Anne Wilson Schaef wrote. And I knew deep down inside my own life that she was right, that our world, too, cannot grow until it changes. I wrote,

> I am still becoming: I am becoming myself—independent, different, free. Those are dangerous, unacceptable, qualities. They violate groupness. And yet, without this kind of change, can we possibly die adults? My problem is that this kind of change came so late and more in response to rejection than to process. But whatever the circumstances, the leap was worth it. I am not the person I was before. I am changed forever.

When conversion comes for both men and women—when women are able to stand on their own and men are able to receive a woman's word, then both men and women will finally be free of the false definition of self that limits them.

The initial question remains, Should men be on the committee? And the answer must surely be: Only if each of them has already become more than what the world tells them that they are.

Chapter Twenty

THE CHURCH AND WOMEN: SPEAKING IN THE NAME OF GOD

And in those days I will pour out my spirit on my servants. Both men and women; and they shall prophesy.

—Acts 2:18

Indeed the time has come: women everywhere are prophesying. But are they talking to anybody but themselves? Is anyone listening at all? And if so, why do so many churches, boards, governments still look the way they do? And why and how does the Catholic Church still believe that God talks only to men, is configured only in men, is mediated only by men? Why is the church as sexist as the men who preach this male God? And why do we—I—continue to align myself with an institution so closed, so heretical, so sinful? Because Jesus stayed in the synagogue until the synagogue threw him out, that's why.

—Joan Chittister, Journal, May 23

Rome sweats in August. The sirocco, hot winds that blow through the city from Africa, whips dust into your eyes as you push against it, cooling nothing. So, on this particular day, the cool of the marble, the high ceilings, and dark halls and shuttered windows of the Vatican felt more humane than intimidating. Most of all, I admired the man with whom I was to meet. Cardinal Eduardo Pironio, Argentinian spokesperson for the poor, had been brought to Rome because there had been death threats made against his life. Like Jeremiah, whom King Ahab called "that trouble-maker of Israel" and Jesus, whom both Romans and high priests considered a rabble-rouser, Pironio spoke a truth the Argentinian government did not want to know. He was a man who could hear the poor of the world. So, he could hear women, too. And I told him our truth. I told him about our frustration over documents that defined women's lives, but never asked for either our input or our response. I told him what it felt like to be invisible in the church, of all places. I told him about the increasing alienation of women in the church.

His deep dark eyes were sad. There was no doubt he understood. But then he dropped his shoulders, clasped his hands between his knees and began to shake his head slowly from side to side. "Jhoan, Jhoan, Jhoan," he said. "What you say is true but you must never say it any place but here. For the sake of the church," he said, "you must never say these things in public. Only here"—he gestured around the room—"only here behind closed doors, between ourselves."

I understood his concerns. I know as well as he did that unity is a fragile strength. But I also knew what he didn't. For the sake of the church, what women wanted had to be said in public because there was nowhere else for a woman to say it. Other than a few token women whose presence is designed to deceive us as to who really has the power, no women ever get behind the closed doors where the final draft of church documents are written, or the pronouns are determined, or the committees are chosen, or the boards are set up. But if the best of them, if a Pironio, couldn't see that, then I knew that to stay in this church was going to take a special kind of spiritual strength. Years later, I saw that conversation and that conclusion mirrored over and over again in the journal. Nothing had changed.

The spirituality demanded at a time of tension in the church itself requires more than patience. "Time changes nothing," the proverb teaches. "People do." But while we work for change, we need a spirituality of conviction, honesty, awareness, endurance, and faith in the God whose time is not our time.

Conviction, the sure, clear notion that something needs to be righted, does not make the long haul possible; it makes it imperative. "To imagine the Divine Feminine, is to meet a deeply felt need. It is also to turn our priorities topsy-turvy," Connie Zweig reminded me. "Deeply-felt need" is what conviction is all about. I wrote in return,

> For a woman to be free, God can no longer be male only. As long as we are nothing but handmaidens of a male god, we cannot possibly become the adult, full, human beings that the God of life meant us to be. For that to happen we must be able to see ourselves, too, in the image of God.

The conviction that the loss of the feminine dimension of God leaves women disadvantaged and spiritually subordinate or inferior everywhere challenges spirituality as we know it.

That conviction is larger than ourselves. It has something to do with reclaiming a whole spiritual life for everyone, man or woman. "The image of God as Mother of the whole creation . . . is an image of inclusive love," Judith Plaskow and Carol P. Christ wrote. And I knew the truth of it in the center of my soul. It is the conviction that to have been given the image of half a god means that both women and men will be crippled by it. That conviction drives me on. I wrote,

> I want a God who is "Mother." I am tired of the finger-shaking, law-giving Father-God who wears a miter and a ring. I want a God who is pregnant energy, bearer of life. My life. Directly. Not my life mediated only by men who exclude women because "God" tells them to do it and, because of which, they "have no authority to change it."

But that kind of honesty is dangerous. Honesty requires that we touch the truth within ourselves and say it out loud so that the Holy Spirit can work in us all. Truth that is suppressed is truth denied to the theological enterprise. It limits the idea of God. And the God who can be thought of cannot possibly be God. But if women do not question the contorting of God into maleness, do not share their own notions of God, then we doom ourselves to nonidentity and men to heterodoxical arrogance. "If women's stories are not told, the depth of women's souls will not be known," Carol Christ whispered in my ear when I least wanted to hear it. I wrote in return:

> It is so true that the Great Silence has scattered and confused and destroyed and isolated women. I have, in small ways, tried to raise a chorus of those who will not succumb to the lies of their existence. But it is not easy. Even women believe, so clever has the propaganda been, that women are supposed to suffer. Silently.

And so many women choose to deny the obvious. Like blacks who believed in the inferiority their masters told them of themselves and so never left the plantations, women have for long ignored the truth in themselves in order to avoid the pain of knowing. A spirituality of awareness calls us to examine every facet of our spiritual lives to determine what God expects of women as women, rather than wait to be told by men what men expect of women. As Audre Lorde put it, "As women, we need to examine the ways in which our world can be truly different."

Have no doubt about it, however: Once we admit to ourselves that something does not feel right about what they have told us about our relationship to God, that awareness becomes our cross. We begin to see into everything, everywhere. And it is not always a pretty picture, even in the church. For instance, I set out to write about the biblical story of Ruth, thinking I would find the story of women's friendship. When I got into the book, however, I discovered that it wasn't really about the relationship between Ruth and Naomi, at all. And it certainly wasn't about Boaz. It was much larger than any of that. It was about Ruth's relationship as a woman to the world and to God. I wrote in response to Lorde,

> I am deep into the writing of *The Story of Ruth.* It is opening up for me a whole new way to look at a woman's life and her needs. It is also making me look again at the way men have exegeted Scripture for us all our lives. Ruth they have made a story about Boaz! Typical. It's enough to make me think about writing another "woman's bible" myself! What do they know about us and why do they never ask!?

Awareness is a blessed curse. Better to be blind sometimes than to see.

That's where the spirituality of endurance comes in. Consciousness commits us. Once we begin to see, we can never not see again, which means that we must be able to bear the burdens of our knowledge. We have to keep going back to touch the tradition, the history, the hope that lies in the sight of Jesus raising a woman from the dead. The problem is that you will get tired of telling it.

Carroll Saussy wrote, "Women need to tell their stories and they need to be heard." I responded to that one out of years of experience:

> There is no doubt that women need to tell their stories. But at the same time, there comes a time when you are too tired of trying to be heard in a place like the church where no one wants to hear you. Then, you walk out of it, past it, beyond it. And often, invisibly. They think you're still there, because your body is, but your heart is long gone and your spirit free. I know.

Then, whatever the ennui, the downright depression, the fatigue, the doubt, we find ourselves adrift in God. Then, nothing can stop the one who knows that the whole truth has yet to be heard, that the gospel is still being rejected by the very people who are responsible for telling it. It happened over and over again in the life of Jesus. Why not now in ours? The gospel confronts each of us newly every day because each of us comes to it only when the life of Jesus intersects with our own over the same issue at the same time. Little by little, looking at Jesus, we begin to realize that the issues Jesus addressed are with us still. Waiting, this time, to be addressed by us. Little by little we come to see the self-serving postures of institutions, even the best of them, our own obligations to the outcast, our personal blindness, and the politicization of the prophetic. Little by little, for the sake of our daughters and our sons, we become converted ourselves. I wrote one day,

To stop aspiring to the goals and definitions of the male world, was the thing that finally set me free—mind, soul and body. It is God and I alone now, guided by the tradition, informed by the past, but not wedded to either.

Then, the spirituality of faith, lived faith in a living God, makes it possible for us to go the next step in darkness. Surrounded by darkness, we are nevertheless drawn by a light we are convinced must be coming because anything else is only half the story of God's will for the world.

"Keep traveling, Sister! Keep traveling! The road is far from finished," Nelle Morton wrote. I took a deep breath and responded,

Indeed we are not finished. The struggle for women is only just begun actually. But I have come to the conclusion that social change does not happen in a straight line. It's run and coast, run and coast all the way. This is another deceleration period, perhaps. Everything has quieted, slowed for a while, no big demonstrations, no great amount of organizing. But it is precisely now we must not stop or we will stand to lose our hearts along the way.

ECOLOGY:
THE OTHER SIDE
OF THE SPIRITUAL LIFE

Many people find renewal and strength in the presence of Mother earth.

—Elaine M. Ward

Sometimes it is only nature that revives me. I say to myself: There must be purpose in all of this. If this can exist, can bring beauty, can bring shelter, can bring new life, then so may I exist for a purpose beyond me. But all of that is so distant, so foreign to the great dogmatic tomes on which we were raised. Actually, at this point of life, I choose nature as a spiritual director over all the popes in history. Nature I trust to understand and grow me.

—Joan Chittister, Journal, April 22

CHRISTIANITY HAS TAKEN A STRANGE AND DISTORTED bent, one that is more the product of the philosophers, I think, than justified by the life of Jesus. I remember that the Pharisees questioned it: "John fasted," they said. "This one comes eating and drinking." John was an ascetic, in other words. Jesus, on the other hand, drank life to the dregs. He went to parties, played with children, told stories, ate with rich people, fished a little, suffered, and died. He made the flesh real. He valued it enough to raise it from the dead. He did not see material things as either sinful or useless. So, where did we go wrong?

How is it that we could disdain nature and call such pomposity holy? How could we consume the Earth with no reverence for it? How can we possibly explain the fact that we have made the globe a cesspool? Somehow we must account for the human tendency to consume the very things that sustain us and to destroy what we say we love. "Our care giving is important in the universe," Kathy Wonson Eddy's excerpt read. I stopped at the word "care giving." I wrote in return,

The ability to care for others is the only gift we have to give
the world at large. The question, of course, is, What is care?
Is it what we want to do for the other or is it what people
ask us to do for them? Or, on the other hand, is it cultivation of the Earth for my sake or for the sake of the Earth?
Surely those who love us as we want to be loved love us more
than those who love us only on their own terms. What does
that have to do with the way we both live and love? What
does that have to do with being "spiritual people"?

The philosophers, Plato and Aristotle, who lived and
wrote more than several hundred years before Jesus, had already reasoned to a God who was all spirit. Which is fine if
they hadn't concluded then that everything that wasn't all
spirit was useless. As clearly it's not. After all, we are it and
we are here—useful as we can be. And what's more, we're
surrounded by useful things, by natural beauty, by ever-
renewing life that we say comes from the life that is God. So
how can any of it be bad, and if not bad, at least useless to
our spiritual life.

We've been so warped by this compulsion to separate
spirit and nature—as if there weren't a spirit in nature, as in
our own natural selves—that we have made the exclusion of
nature a spiritual thing.

The Native Americans, the Wiccans, the medicine men,
the animists, all of whom felt the power of God in nature,
aligned themselves with it. They slept to its rhythms, worked
to its pace, honored its seasons. They recognized the power
and personality in everything and sought to communicate
with it. They wanted to know the character of it, to understand the power of it, to embrace the energy of it. They
learned the way of nature from everything around them. In
the totems they built out of aspects of the animal world,
they described themselves and their needs, their fears and

their ideals. They mounted the eagle for daring and the owl for wisdom and the fox for cunning and the bear for strength. They saw themselves in everything and everything in themselves. They immersed themselves in the spirit of the universe and knew themselves to be one with it.

Then we came along. Civilized.

We defined matter as "inert" and animal and plant life as "irrational." We made ourselves the highest good of natural things and forgot the God of nature. We lost touch with the universe and became a universe unto ourselves.

Only a remnant of the bridge between the human and the divine remains in us: The sacramental system reminds us at every stage of our existence that the God of life touches us through the most mundane of things: through water and fire, oil and light, incense and flowers, bread and wine, salt and the touch of the other. It reminds us of the essential goodness—the godness, in fact—of the natural world. It doesn't teach us that nature is God or that God is nature. It teaches us that God comes to us through the natural because nature was created by God. Or at least it tries to teach us our immersion in life. When we allow it.

But every once in a while, a spirituality of negation sweeps across the spiritual world, warping our sense of the holy and making holiness itself a commitment to the unnatural. Extreme asceticism captures the spiritual imagination, and a spirituality of death consumes us. We beat ourselves with whips and chains. We deprive our bodies of water and wheat. We separate ourselves from beauty and art. We even assume the negative effect of the other on our own spiritual lives.

We feared the body. We feared comfort. We feared that joy would weaken us. "Remember, Joan," my mother said, "if you go to a convent, you won't be able to come home from school and curl up on the couch the way you do now." And she was right. I thought it was silly then. After all, what was wrong with couches? I think it's silly now for anyone to assume that holiness is that easy. Holiness requires the cultivation of the soul, not the derogation of the body.

All of that disdain of the self, the flesh, the beauty of the world around us, might be all right. I mean, if some people want to live in the world as if they aren't here, who are we to try to stop them? But if that attitude toward nature in ourselves is universalized to imply that the bounty of nature around us—as Bacon said in his justification for the scientific method—"is to be bound into service like a slave," then we run the risk of sinning against the planet, the universe, and all its peoples. How else do we explain the way we rape our rain forests, pollute our rivers, burn holes in the ozone layer, suck the world's natural habitats dry of oil, and threaten nuclear war? How can we possibly justify such things other than that we have lost all sense, not only of the presence of God in nature, but of the synchronicity of the self with nature as well. The end of such thinking—that matter is useless, that the flesh is bad, that spirit is all—spawns a spirituality of negation. We punish the body and strip the Earth. And we do it in pursuit of a so-called holiness that smacks of the bogus, that denies the gifts of God, that makes us marauders on the earth.

"God has made everything that is made, and God loves everything that God has made," Julian of Norwich wrote. The quotation struck me deeply. I began to think of how I have been tainted, too, by this cult of human superiority. I had assumed that nature was for my use, that I could swallow it whole, that I owed it no regard, that humans were its master—as if to live outside the laws of nature would not eventually destroy humanity itself. As it is doing right now.

Worst of all, I had been made to believe that some humans were more human than other humans. Some humans, even, were better than other humans. Some of us were in charge of the rest of us, and we knew who we were. I had learned that some humans, therefore, could do anything they wanted to other human beings less fully human than themselves—like blacks and Jews and women. I wrote,

> So, if Julian is right, what can we—what of life, of nature, can I—possibly reject? But I do. At least at the feeling level. If I follow this thinking to the end, then to harm anything is to confront the love of God. Note the word "harm." I can resist it, yes—even reject it, maybe—but I may not harm it because God loves it. Given the way we live on this earth, the thought boggles the mind.

It is surely this rupture from nature, this assumption that higher life is more worthy life, and this audacious tendency to rank everything according to its fullness of life, as we define it—from rocks to humans, from darkest to lightest skinned, from woman to man—that leads us to subdivide even humanity itself into categories of human, more human, most human. With ourselves at the top of the pyramid. But if we believe that God built inequality into the human race, then we can do anything we want to do with anything "lower" than we are on the scale of superiority we create for ourselves. Then we are only a step away from the lynching of black people, the extermination of red people, the napalming of yellow people, and someday surely, if we do not come to wholeness as a species, to the gassing of the next generation of Jews.

"Just as we are sustained physically by the food we eat, we are also sustained spiritually, moment by moment, as often as we eat, as often as we drink," Jean Blomquist wrote. And I answered,

> I realize, of course, that Blomquist must surely be referring to the fact that not to feed the body is to threaten the spirit, as well. I'm not sure that it is food that sustains the spirit—in more than the physical sense—but I do believe that the spirit must be sustained. The spirit that is not nurtured dies. The spirit needs great doses of nature, of love, of thought, of poetry, of ideas, of mystery and ritual and prayer. When any of those go, the spirit goes, too.

There is no doubt about it: Ecology is an essential element of the spiritual life. And if we are not converted to it soon enough, it may well be too late.

Chapter Twenty-One

NATURE:
THE VOICE OF GOD AROUND US

Flowers are my metaphor for God reminding us that our lives are fragile and precious.

—Alexandra Stoddard

I have come to understand that the voice of God is all around me. God is not a silent God. God is speaking to me all the time. In everything. Through everyone. I am only now beginning to listen, let alone to hear. In bare trees, I hear God saying that it is possible to die over and over again and yet survive. In the stones of this Irish landscape, I hear God saying that there is nothing that can't be endured. Not the storm, not the wind, not even the passage of time.

—Joan Chittister, Journal, August 30

FOUR OF US LIVE IN AN OLD GEORGIAN HOUSE IN THE middle of the inner city, the site of our first foundation in Erie. The monastery, founded in 1856, was at the center of the German immigrant community of the era, which is why the Benedictine Sisters of Erie—the mission of a German abbey—settled there in the first place. The Germans moved up in society eventually and moved on. The area itself remained a basically transient area, however. The neighborhood found itself host to one immigrant population after another—the Irish, the Polish, the blacks, the Vietnamese, the Hispanic, and now the Russians. So the community stayed there in the middle of the inner city, where resources are scarce and the living areas deteriorate rapidly.

It's a typical inner-city neighborhood: a warren of wellworn old places, down at the heels, but clinging to pride. The house we live in had only one owner before us. The family had come to the area about the same time the community did, built their house next door to the monastery, and raised generation after generation of children in that house. In 1989, the last remaining survivor of the family moved away. Better not to have a crack house that near to small children, we decided, so we bought the place as a kind of buffer for our day care center next door.

It's a gracious house of old red brick, built tall and thin and plain. But the best thing about it is that it has a secret.

Behind the house there is a sunken garden full of shrubs and bushes and flower beds and a rose garden and a gnarled old beech tree and one forty-foot spruce that towers above the tenements behind it—as out of place, and so, as beautiful a thing in the inner city as you will ever see.

Sister Mary has tended that garden ever since the day we moved in. She does it, she says, in honor of the women we had watched weed and water it for years. They're gone now, but what they did year after year, one plant at a time, thrives on.

The important thing about the garden, though, is that no one can see it from the street. Only the people in the tenements above it can watch the flowers grow. A pity, we think. But there is something magical about the fact that it is there, nevertheless. Just blooming, secretly, year after year. Just there. Being.

Oh, she's added a few things from year to year—more roses, the wisteria bush, tulips—but by and large, the garden is still the garden of the first women that planted it, a reminder of how life goes on if it's well tended. I sit at the breakfast table, in what we call somewhat pompously The Garden Room, because it overlooks the rose bushes, and think.

Like the garden, much of what we do is perennial. Most of what we do grows up in us before we even realize it. Few people know about it but us. In fact, quiet growth is what most of life is all about. And what is planted in one time grows up in us in another.

"We are energized and empowered by the 'green-ness' of God's love," Kathleen Crockford Ackley's entry read. And she was right, at least about me and my life. I wrote back after a long, slow period of emotional hibernation and personal uncertainty,

> I feel "green" again and I am convinced that is a sign that the Spirit of God is alive in me. I feel like I have finally come to that period, that place in life that I was meant to come to all the time. The teaching, the administration were all nothing but necessary periods of pruning along the way. I learned from them, of course, but they were never the real end point of my life.

All of life's twists and turns are all there for the reading in the garden of the soul. If only we will.

Life is not lived on a continuum. Not even the spiritual life. We do not find God on a laser beam, bright and cold and straight. We have times of great, dark incubation. We have times that are barren and arid and bleak. We go through periods when life feels more like death than like gestation. But it is always gestating. It may even be in the dark times that we grow the most. "Springtime God . . . we need your persistent love to disturb . . . our heart's rigidity," Kate Compston wrote. I had been grappling with the need in me for a "once and for all" resolution of events and ideas for a long time. I wanted life to get right and stay that way. After all, I had been working on some of those things for years. Wasn't it time to see some results, to finish one thing so we could get on with the next? I wrote,

> I love the image of a "springtime God." Isn't God always in the growing season in us? Isn't everything that happens in life simply seeding something to come—and isn't all of it God? But if that's true, the question is, then, Are all our thoughts new seeds of life to be pursued? Because if so, then I am being called on and I am, as usual, reluctant to go.

I watch the garden come and go year after year. I don't know a thing about flowers or bushes or shrubs to this day. But I know when the back part of the garden will go white. And the front part will go bright orange. And the leaves on the rare old beech will turn gold. Each of them touches something different in me. Each of them releases something in me that nothing else does. I am learning to live my life according to the calendar of that garden. "A wisdom still abides in the natural rhythms of the earth, if we are still and open ourselves to it," Kimberly Greene Angle wrote. I thought of our garden and winced at the thought of the lesson in it that I had not been learning or to which I would not listen. I wrote with a bit of chagrin,

> There is a wisdom in natural rhythm but we long ago abandoned it to technology and electricity. Now there is no stopping, no ending. Only quitting. I long ago fell prey to it

and forgot how to stop and wondered how to quit. So now two unnatural rhythms try for the marrow of my soul: fatigue that is chronic and frustration that is terminal. I am determined to defeat them both.

We have become human hamsters on a twenty-four-hour wheel. We work and run and talk at all times. The dark never overtakes us. The silence of the day never sets in. And we wonder why we can't find God. We are never still enough anymore to listen to the voice within that will tell us how. We fail to understand that every season of life has a message of its own for us. We want bland and steady, certain and successful, over challenge and hope, trust and faith. I wrote on the same subject in another place:

> My God is definitely a God of the seasons. I prefer that God in spring and fall—when things emerge and things mellow—but I have learned more from the God who is the heat of my day and the icy obstacles of my life. From that God I have learned the depths of the self.

I don't do "nature" the way other people do. I'm not a hiker or a gardener or a biker for a lot of reasons—some of them physical, some of them personal. There's a picture of me at the age of fifteen sitting in a tree at the edge of the lake, yes, but I'm reading. I only went up there to get away from the volleyball enthusiasts who would certainly have pressed me into service otherwise. I much preferred poetry to spiking a ball. And I did go fishing regularly, but that was because in that capacity I could do both: set the line and read at the same time. But I've learned an enormous amount about life from our garden, hopefully not too late to have it count. Gardens have a way of reminding us that death is never forever, no matter what it is that we think we've lost. "All shall be well, and all shall be well, and all manner of things shall be well," Julian of Norwich wrote. I've come to believe in the truth of that. I wrote,

> It is learning to believe that in the end "all shall be well" that may really be the central task of life. I must believe that this empty, rudderless, barren, unsuccessful time is really part of the process. I must come to realize that all of life is part of the beauty of life. Otherwise, in the desire to be somewhere else, I may miss where I am—and what I am, as well.

Getting back in touch with nature may be the only real cure for the agitated soul.

Chapter Twenty-Two

CREATION:
THE PROCESS THAT NEVER ENDS

If we come to terms with our history, we free ourselves to move to-ward a better future.

—Janet Kalven and Mary I. Buckley

How would I ever "come to terms with my history"? As in put it aside as if it had nothing to do with my future. How would I "make sense" of two such different lives? The first as an only child with a dead father, a mixed marriage, an alzheimer's mother, an alcohol-dependent stepfather, and an institutionalized existence since the age of sixteen underlies another whole life entirely. The second life, this one, has been rich, kind, good, meaningful, steeped in God, and crowded with people of quality. So the first one couldn't have been that bad, could it? Somehow, it must have prepared me quite well, in fact, for the rest of life. Clearly, we cannot too quickly cross off anything in life. It all goes into the pattern at the end.

—Joan Chittister, Journal, September 15

THE THING ABOUT CREATION, THE SPIRITUAL TRADITION teaches, is that God makes something out of nothing. Unfortunately, most of us forget that we're it. Whatever we become as the years go by comes out of the nothingness with which we started. Life itself presents the raw material of our shaping, not ourselves. We do not come into this world full-blown. We come in becoming, and we go on becoming all our lives.

We like to think of ourselves as "finished," of course. We have high-water marks to assure us of that, and we count them off: our first day in school, First Communion, Confirmation, first driver's license, high school graduation, first paycheck, and twenty-first birthday, which signals our adulthood. But it doesn't work. Every day thereafter we do nothing but discover in ourselves what's missing, what's confusing, what we don't know.

Rita was young and competitive and angry. Very angry. She was brighter than most, she knew, but no one ever elected her to anything. She rolled her eyes to show the rest of the group how impatient she was with the inadequacy of the process. Or the incompetence of the chairperson. Then, years later, she found herself in charge of a major project. Now she became the target; she became the person whose process people judged or whose plans failed to satisfy. She doesn't roll her eyes as much anymore.

Paul was a young priest who had been seduced by his own clerical collar. He couldn't remember the name of the woman who had been the parish secretary for eighteen years. He loved to write letters for the bulletin that started, "I have ordered that. . . . " He reminded everyone always of just who and what he saw himself to be. Then the pedophilia scandal broke in the church. Paul's not a priest anymore. They say he lives a very quiet life selling shoes. They also say that he's a much nicer man to talk to now.

I had an aunt who married for the third time at the age of seventy-five. She lived six months in the United States and six months in New Zealand so her husband wouldn't lose his pension. She flew back and forth at will. I never saw her look healthier or happier than she did then.

All of these people changed. All of them became another part of themselves. In all of them, creation went on creating.

It takes a while to understand how creation happens. It takes living. Creation is not so simple as simply growing up. It requires us to grow down, to grow in, to grow beyond, as well. "It is through our human experience that we meet God," Elaine Ward wrote. And remembering the years full of people whose presence had molded my life, some softly, some like steel, I wrote,

> It takes a lifetime to really understand that God is in what is standing in front of us. Most of our lives are spent looking, straining to see the God in the cloud, behind the mist, beyond the dark. It is when we face God in one another, in creation, in the moment, that the real spiritual journey begins.

Parts of the spiritual tradition deludes us into thinking that God resides somewhere high above humanity, too "other" to be sullied by it. The task of holiness, this school implies, lies in avoiding the debasing things of this world in order to qualify for the next. The name of the game is the diminishment of the self for the sake of the preeminence of God. "God must increase; I must decrease"—the Baptist's response to the fact that Jesus is now baptizing too—becomes distorted over time to imply that the self must be suppressed to accommodate union with God. Since God is everything, this interpretation implies, I must be nothing. But that's a strange theology. It means that what the All Good Creator made is not worthy of the Creator.

The whole idea of the worthlessness of the human being began to be debunked by the modern world's recognition of the uniqueness and value of the individual. In the eighteenth and nineteenth centuries, with the development of the industrial age and the emergence of the nuclear family, childhood became recognized for the first time as a separate stage of life and even children began to be treated as persons.

The process of individuation sharpened not only our respect for the other, but it led us to pay attention to the movements in our own hearts, as well. Then, learning to understand our own motives and needs and selves, we came to understand those around us as well. Coming to value the undeveloped self within, we saw the undeveloped other in a new light. Self, we began to realize, is the filter through which we see the world. What we know of ourselves we apply to the other. What we deny to ourselves we deny to the other. What we believe to be the origin and end of the self, we know to be the origin and end of the other. The very survival of the human race rests on our commitment to the spirit of God in human nature, in ourselves, in the other. "Human dignity is no other than the respect due to the image of God in us," Mercy Oduyoye wrote. The clarity of it shatters us. What took us so long to see it. I wrote,

> Because God is in us, we have dignity. No other reason. None at all. So, to fail to touch that part of ourselves is to give that part of ourselves away. And yet, what is it that nurtures the sense of God in us when all of life is geared to control us rather than to free us to be ourselves. I wonder if it is possible to outgrow the tendency to be less than the fullness of ourselves.

To suppress the development of the individual for the sake of some faceless, nameless virtue—humility, obedience, self-control—may do more to stamp out the God-life within us than it does to bring it to life.

The problem, of course, is that we fail. We know ourselves to be weak. We stumble along, being less than we can be, never living up to our own standards, let alone anyone else's. We eat too much between meals, we work too little to get ahead, we drink more than we should at the office party. We're all addicted to something. Those addictions not only cripple us, they convince us that we are worthless and incapable of being worthwhile. It is a self-fulfilling prophecy of the worst order because it traps us inside our own sense of inadequacy, of futility, of failure.

For Frankie, my handsome, young Eagle Scout cousin, the addiction was to marijuana. Maybe more, no one's really sure. He gave it up, they say, but not before he lost his tall blond wife and his three-year-old son. So, on Christmas Eve he broke into the church where he had served Mass as a child to pray a while. Then he went home, took his father's hunting rifle out of the gun cupboard, locked himself in his bedroom, and put a bullet through his head. At twenty-two. How is it that we failed to teach this young man so little about God, about growth, about falling and getting up again, about the long, slow process of creation? How could he think so little of himself? And, most of all, how is it that the rest of us think the same, unless it's because we do not trust the God of creation?

"A God who cannot feel cannot be alive and intimately related to other lives," Joanne Carlson Brown and Rebecca Parker said. The statement has a great deal to say about what we think about creation, its purpose, and its end. If God the Creator is a pitiless minder of purely mechanical creatures who jump through hoops, fail, and are disposed of casually, creation is simply the cruel exercise of a cruel God. But life doesn't feel that way. Life deals with us kindly in most instances. We become desperately ill and then recover. We flounder at one thing and succeed outrageously at others. We miss the mark in one place and wind up better off for it in the end. The human heart knows better what God is than any books can ever tell.

After a lifetime of struggling through failures, of my own and of those around me, whose feelings of shame and fear and self-hatred I could not assuage, I wrote,

> The God of wrath and recrimination is a God who does not understand the creatures She herself has borne. This God is no God at all. On the contrary, we are the breath of a God who delights in our efforts to be more than we are despite the fact we can't be more than we are. For what is human development if not the search for what we cannot reach, the desire for what we cannot be—and the certainty that in the end we will be everything God ever intended us to be. And we know that, because this desire for wholeness is built into us by God.

A true spirituality of creation, one that does not see creation as a single finished point in time, gives us the right to grow. It implies not only a God who made us, but a God who is with us, in us, and in everything around us. Whoever we are, whatever we are, this God knows us, understands us, walks with us to the melting point where what we are and what God is become one.

The purpose of life is to lead us from one small shrine to another, until, finally, there are no more spurious idols between us and the God who is really our God. Then creation is over. Then we're not "finished," perhaps, but we are ready to begin. "The God who made the world and everything in it, being Sovereign of heaven and earth, does not live in shrines made by human hands," Acts 17:24 reads. I understood the statement only too well. I wrote, knowing the place and purpose of all the shrines of my life, but aware now not only of how temporary they were, but of how temporary they were meant to be,

> This, of course, is the great truth, and I have spent most of my life learning it. First I thought God was in a shrine called "The Catholic Church" and I worshiped it accordingly. It was a fault as much mine as it was theirs. A scintilla of history read with an open heart would have proven it. Then, in a later stage, I thought God was in a shrine called the Erie Benedictines. I gave that shrine my all and worshiped it, too, until time disabused me of that false God, as well. God was beyond even that. Now I am finding God everywhere and taking the divine wherever I find it, sure that if this temple falls, God will be for me on the other side of these walls, too. It is a great liberation.

The God of creation goes on creating us. The danger is that we ourselves are inclined to call our creation over before its time.

DAILINESS: THE GIFTS OF THE MUNDANE

God restores my soul. God leads me in paths of righteousness for God's name's sake.

—Psalm 23:3

When I am feeling battered by life—sometimes even by life at its best—I take a deep breath and remember that though God is in all of it, God is also greater than all of it. Then both what I lose in the battering and what I become because of it are simply chances to be more of the real thing, to become more than the thing itself. At the end of everything is God.

—Joan Chittister, Journal, March 14

CRISES WE'RE GOOD AT. IT'S DAILINESS THAT GETS US down. When word comes of the illness or the accident or the danger, we set our faces to the wind, hunch our shoulders, and move steadfastly ahead. The spiritual challenge of dealing with the unknown channels our spiritual resources as much as it raises our adrenaline. We begin to talk about having faith. We remember what trust is about. We start to pray again. We ask for mercy and forgiveness and help. And somehow, we weather the storm. Clearly, it's not crises that kill us. It's the long and bitter stress of holding the course after the storm dies but the current goes on running against us that wears us down. It's the long haul that hurts. Then, the effort of keeping the faith, maintaining the trust, wears thin.

When Jack lost his job for the third year in a row, I hated the thought of having to call him. What do you say to someone who's been dealt such a blow? He was talented, experienced, and very highly thought of in the field. He'd be shattered.

I wasn't prepared for the conversation I'd dreaded to have. The fact is that Jack sounded positively buoyant on the phone. Yes, it had been a shock. Sure, it was a blow. But these things happen, he said. What's more, he was sure that this had all happened for a purpose. "God," he assured me, "must have bigger things in mind" for him now. But not really. What he thought would bring great change to his life turned out to be simply more of the same.

Jack got a new job in a new company, of course, but he found himself doing what he'd done all his professional life. Not long after, Jack began to change. He went to work every day, but he was sour and listless. There was no spirit in the clay. It wasn't catastrophe he couldn't handle; it was dailiness that taxed him to the limit. Life had not left him destitute; life had left him bored. What is the spiritual value in that?

Dailiness tests the mettle of the self. The ability to go back to the same task, day after day after day—taking care of the children, doing the shopping, hawking a product, stacking the shelves—with new attention to the task, with new concern for the outcome, takes a special kind of faith, another kind of trust.

Having worked in a counseling relationship with people for almost thirty years, I know the problem. It's not long before a good counselor knows the rest of the story after the first paragraph of the first interview. A great counselor, on the other hand, isn't listening for the scenario; there are only so many of those in the world. A great counselor goes beyond the facts to listen keenly for the way this very mundane situation affected this particular person and why. And there are no two alike of those in the world. It's learning to bring your whole self to something that makes the difference between a happy life and a dull life, a holy life and an empty one.

Life is not made up of crises; life is made up of little things we love to ignore in order to get on to the exciting things in life. But God is in the details. God is in what it takes in us to be faithful to them. God is in the routines that make us what we are. The way we do the little things in life is the mark of the bigness of our souls. "When the mundane things that occupy our time threaten to dull our view of the universe, it is time to slow down," Madeline McClenney-Sadler wrote. But after years of stimulation, I know the beauty of the routine. I wrote back,

> The "mundane" is certainly dull, I agree, and may even limit us—not only our perceptions but even the breadth of our questions. At the same time, there is something very freeing, very humanizing about the mundane. Doing dishes and buying vegetables get us back in touch with ourselves, give us time to smell the earth of our lives, give us time just to be. We will go on long after the big ideas fade and the profession ends. The question is, Will there be anything in me then? Will there be a me in me? It all depends on how I deal with the mundane.

The problem with dailiness is that it's not nearly as routine as it's supposed to be. It takes patience and persistence. It takes a willingness to give of ourselves beyond what our role descriptions demand. It requires us to pour ourselves out, not to store ourselves up for our own satisfaction.

I lived in a residence hall once where the accountant doubled as receptionist. Except that she would never look up at anyone at the desk. And when you did cough enough to annoy her into action, she punished you for it by refusing to find the forms you needed so you wouldn't ask again. It happens everywhere—and we know it. I have watched parents relegate their children to a set of TV cartoons rather than talk to them. And I have felt the irritation of having all my own grand plans consumed by someone else's agenda for me. Then I read Katherine Paterson's entry in the journal one day. Paterson wrote, "As I look back on what I have written, I can see that the very persons who have taken away my time and space are those who have given me something to say." Having been so irritated by interruptions so often, I could feel the back of my neck get hot as I wrote,

> To think of your interruptions as your education is a wonderful attitude to have. I must come to see in my own life that the mail that comes, the people who call, the meetings that happen, the children who erupt in the center of our lives are all grist for my mill. As it is, I am always trying to escape them.

Indeed on the subject of the spirituality of the daily and the way it taxes the soul, I am an expert.

We were taught in second grade that the stranger who knocks at the door in the middle of the night could well be the Christ in disguise. Years later, I discovered, the Rule of Benedict insists that someone be kept on the door both day and night in order to "welcome the pilgrim and the stranger, to receive the guest as Christ." The older I get, the more I am convinced that there is nothing wrong with that theology. God is in the fine points. God is hidden in public view of us. God is where we are, calling us to be the Christ there. Otherwise, what is the presence of God in us supposed to be about?

But perhaps the hardest part of the spirituality of dailiness is having faith enough to deal with the discouragement that comes with finding ourselves trapped in a moment that never ends. In that one long, drawn-out moment of sadness, disquietude, frustration, rejection that comes into every life and has a way of staying, sometimes for years, can lie the most arduous moments of the spiritual life. "Who will roll away the stone for us from the entrance to the tomb?" Janet

Ross-Heiner wrote, as if in memory only of one tomb long gone and not mine. But I've seen people in tombs called marriages, called failure, called depression, called ennui. And I have known a few tombs myself. I wrote in reply to that idea,

> There are so many stones at the tomb of my heart these years. I went through life enmeshed in one external struggle after another—family, health, money, rejection—but only in the last ten years have I known the pain of having to hang on for no clear reason at all to a life of shards going nowhere while the sun shines on the opposite mountain.

It's the dailiness of the tomb that really calls for faith, for trust, for perseverance and persistence. We want to live in resurrection all our lives, but it is the waiting time that makes us worthy of it.

It's when we go on in the heat of the noonday sun that we know what it is like to walk the dusty roads of Galilee. It's when we go on without firecrackers or music that we understand what the desert is like. It's when we go on despite the fact that quitting would be more satisfying that we know that God has taken control of our lives. Then, we are being used for something greater than ourselves. Then, we are being used to bring the world around us to fullness. It's licking the stamps and taking down the chairs and making the callbacks that finally, finally change the world. And that is the spirituality of dailiness.

Dailiness is the great deep pit out of which the character of our lives takes its most lasting shape. It is the repository of our greatest graces and site of our worst losses. It is the treasure house of all our yesterdays and the reserve out of which we draw strength for all our tomorrows. "Your love for me, O God, is like the deepness of a well," Nancy Nelson Elsenheimer wrote. It made such sense to me. This one I understood in an instant:

> I like this image of God's love "like the deepness of a well." What is to be remembered is that that image also implies that God's love for us is black and dark and not able to be seen into completely. And I know for sure that's true. How explain as "love" a ruptured home life, an unhealthy novitiate, a dying institution, a lost future, a lack of personal freedom. And yet it has been love unending, love without bounds. Would I have designed it that way? Well, in a sense I did, didn't I? I decided daily how to handle it. And God has been with me every step of the way.

Dailiness is what makes us fully and finally what we really are.

Chapter Twenty-Three

STRUGGLE:
THE SEARCH FOR GOD IN DARKNESS

God offers rivers in the deserts of our arid lives.

—Lavon Bayler

I need a river in the desert right now: a cool, deep, clear running river. I need something to show me that this is the right work and the right way. It has been almost ten years of wandering, of feeling rootless, useless, and mediocre. If only something would happen to say that these years have been worth it. God of Rivers, come.

—Joan Chittister, Journal, July 15

EVERYBODY SUFFERS IN LIFE. WE ALL KNOW WHAT IT'S like either to be depressingly sick ourselves or to have someone we love die or to lose everything we've worked for overnight. We all know periods of real stress. But though everyone suffers, not everyone has a life of suffering. David did.

David grew up in a family of eight children whose alcoholic father plunged them deeper and deeper into poverty every year. His mother was a sickly woman, toothless and skinny in an affluent world. Two of his younger brothers lived confined to wheelchairs with muscular dystrophy.

His father sobered up, finally, and repented his life. But he died too soon after the conversion to make the repentance real for the rest of the family. There was no time, no way, to make up to the children the childhood they'd missed. The younger brothers and sisters moved on in life. The mother, exhausted for years, eventually gave up completely and died. And David, still a young man himself, woke up one morning to find himself left with two sick brothers to support. One was a long-suffering, pleasant soul, the other an angry, bitter fellow who saw to it that the rest of the world suffered for his suffering. Both of the boys fought the idea of going into a residential center. That left David to do the nursing and the cooking and the shopping and the earning and the errands. David never married. He was already wedded to everything he could handle.

What a terrible life, we say. But I knew David, and the truth is that David was a peaceful, happy man. David clearly knew something about suffering that all of us must come to understand if we are ever to live life fully ourselves. David knew that suffering is not an object. Some people are paralyzed for life and yet live very full lives. They do not "suffer," in the medical sense of the word. David knew that other people have everything—and suffer deeply. Why? Because suffering is what we name it. Suffering is what we are called to transform into new life. Suffering leads us to be another part of ourselves.

But we do not adjust to suffering automatically, like we adjust to breathing. There is a process involved in suffering that leads to liberation.

Suffering is simply one more stage of life that depends more on how we handle it than it does on the circumstances themselves. "In the midst of profound suffering, God is present and new life is possible," Marie Fortune's item in the journal read. And no stranger to suffering myself, like anybody else in life, I struggled with the very concept of struggle. I wrote,

> Why is God in suffering? Maybe because, in those moments, there is little of anything else there. Friends give false consolation, systems ignore us, groups go on unaware, uninterested in our small pain. Only in God can we come to see the broader view, the real purpose of suffering. Suffering pares us to the core, strips us of our complacencies, tears away the gossamer nets on which we depend—and leaves us naked of ourselves. Suffering exposes us to ourselves.

Suffering, it seems, has something to teach us. It is admitting that we have something to learn from it that finally enables us to grow.

The problem is that suffering plunges us into the center of ourselves. It is a dark and lonely journey. It demands that we put down everything we ever counted on to protect us from the coarseness of life. It takes away our security blankets and throws us back on our own resources, often untapped, even unknown, before this time. We cry a lot. We slip into self-pity. We wriggle and strain against the learnings of the moment. We do everything we can to avoid the unavoidable. But if we have the faith for the journey, we come eventually to the raw material of the self. It is the journey every one of us takes alone. No matter what we would hope for otherwise. "We must learn to listen to, hold, and support others for their empowerment and ours," Rita Nakashima Brock wrote. But I was deep into transition from one moment in life to the next. I abided at that point in the universe of the soul that is populated by the self alone. I wrote,

> I can hardly respond to this particular quotation. It sticks in my throat. The fact is that I feel that I "listened and held

and supported and empowered people" for years. And drained myself dry in the process. Then I found myself basically alone at the end of it. No, I am not into "listening, holding, or empowering" now. I am into recovering my own life. Yet. As in, maybe I haven't begun.

One of the major dimensions of suffering is this experience of loneliness that accompanies it, the feeling of being in orbit, without anchors, with no idea of where to go next, with no companions to carry us over. Then, it is a matter of standing still as a fox at the edge of the forest and waiting for life to take another turn. Only then can we begin to build a new world of our own design. Only then do we have options. We can decide to move on, or we can attempt to hold on to a past long gone and, even perhaps, well dead.

The stark reality of the past is not that it was either bad or good. It is simply that it is past. Over. Finished. Yesterday is beyond retrieval. As long as we go on insisting that we will accept nothing less than the past, the present weighs us down. Depression sets in with a vengeance.

Only when we are ready to put down the pain, let what is gone finally go, and stop the fruitless rage, only when we forgo the folly of groundless fear, can we move on. But first we have to trust that the God who brought us to this point will also see us through it.

"God makes me to lie down in green pastures and leads me beside still waters," Psalm 23 reminded me. But I was not ready yet. I wrote,

> I have to believe this scripture fiercely right now because life does not feel like "green pastures" or "still water." It feels like a living death. Everyone around me is still producing, still building, still going on. But I am cut off at the

root with nothing to show for it. I am empty, useless, doing nothing, going nowhere. The speeches and the books flash and fade and I am embarrassed by my existence. So where is God in all of this? What is life without life? I feel like I am on the other side of a window pane looking in and no one sees me. No one is unkind; they are simply uncaring. It is "make your own way time" . . . and I don't know how.

We are defeated. Of all the elements of suffering, it is the grip of defeat that wounds us most. If what we want to have happen never comes, if what we had is gone, we must have done something to deserve it. Or we could have done something to avoid it. Or what we are doing right now is not working. Or it was all for nothing to begin with. Defeat overwhelms us. The struggle is too much.

And worst of all, this new moment in life is simply unacceptable. Instead of accepting what is—the death, the loss, the pain, the confusion—we rail at the world and everything in it. We insist on yesterday and cling to today. We close our minds entirely to tomorrow. We curse the God who has abandoned us. We refuse to believe that the God we seek is with us still. Most of all, we refuse to imagine that in this hurtful, damnable situation echoes the call of God to prod us on beyond where we have been to where we must go if we are ever to be full human beings.

It is the moment of decision. We can allow the pain of loss to curdle us, or we can allow it to push us on beyond the present to the future to which we are being called. We can balk and die in place, or we can allow ourselves to trust the darkness that is the path to new life. We can give up, or we can allow the pain itself to spur us on. "Let the chaff of my irritation at not having all the answers burn to ash," Kathleen

Crockford Ackley wrote. After years of struggle, I understood the point only too well. I wrote,

> Chaff is what's left in the heart after you work through something major, something impacting, something life-changing. It burns forever as both energy and light. It shows the way to a new kind of living and gives the fuel we need to get us there: In my heart, I carry the chaff of death, domestic tension, years of ministry misplacement, a sexist church, and a period of deep disjunction. But, in the end, every one of those things changed me for the better. It has all been good for me.

Once we know that what was, is over, that what is, is good, and that together they have prepared us for what can be, happiness is a given. Nothing can destroy us. Life is within grasp. God is within reach. It is the moment of spiritual emancipation. Then, we see that what has happened in the past has only prepared us for the present. Then, we discover that the present is meant only to be a bridge to even another tomorrow. Here or hereafter.

Then, faith comes. Real faith. The kind of faith that is based on nothing but yesterday; the kind of hope that remembers that every yesterday has simply been harbinger of an even more grace-filled tomorrow. "God's love goes before us in a way we can never fully name," Anne Carr reminded me. And this time I wrote,

> God's love, in fact, is hardly ever named until it is well over and long gone. I am beginning to wonder whether God's love is ever identifiable on the spot. And, if not, then the question is, Why? Maybe the answer is so that we will learn faith rather than love. Love, after all, is natural. Faith is not.

It's when we learn faith that happiness comes—real happiness, that underlying descant of the soul that tells us over and over again that what is, in some strange, unexplainable way, is good. Most of all, faith tells us that what is, is more than good. It is becoming always better. In ways we never thought possible. And how can that be? Because God's ways are not our ways. It is in the depths of darkness that we learn faith; it is in retrospect that we come to recognize love in darkness.

Chapter Twenty-Four

JOY:
THE GOD WHO LOVES LAUGHTER

Our lives are given a certain dignity by their very evanescence.

—Madeleine L'Engle

I suppose L'Engle means that it is what we enjoy that measures our humanity. That makes sense to me. There is a world of difference between people who enjoy TV wrestling and people who enjoy opera! The fact that we can, in fact, "enjoy" at all is a mark of our humanity. Maybe that's why pain, suffering, sterility of spirit is really "inhumane." I do enjoy life; I have also, however, known too much work and too little pure enjoyment. I have to do something about that.

—Joan Chittister, Journal, June 8

SITTING OUT IN THE MIDDLE OF THE CHANNEL IN A little nineteen-foot fishing boat with ocean freighters and large sailboats passing us on both sides, I remember the wild and crazy joy of it: no desk, no phone, no speeches, no airplanes. Just four of us, a hot sun, an empty fish bucket, a parade of boats, and the rocking of the waves. I cast with all my might, caught the top of the channel light, and, laughing my heart out, cut free just in time to avoid wrapping the next

215

sail in fishing line. Life, bare and simple, is a wonderful thing. How do we learn that? And what does it mean for the spiritual life itself?

We learn it by seeing it, I think. When I was a young sister, in the days before the church had negotiated a kind of truce with the world and the monastery reflected the emotional sterility that that standoff implied, Sister Marie Claire, steadfastly opposed to the suppression of joy in the name of holiness, went to her music room every Sunday afternoon to listen to records of symphonies, scores of operas, collections of piano performances. We didn't go to concerts in those days, and only music teachers were allowed to have record players. She would sit in her rocking chair all afternoon and simply listen. I remember being very moved by the model of such bold and wanton delight in the face of such institutionalized negation of it. The lesson served me well. There are times in life when the only proper response to the dreary and the difficult is to ignore them. The person of hope, the person who knows that God is in the daily, knows joy.

The trick in life is to be able to distinguish the things that give us real joy from those that are simply the conventions of diversion. I go to parties, and I have a great time. But when I am looking for a way to cleanse the palette of my soul, I do other things. "Learn to laugh a little to yourself and with others. Play a little to balance your workload," Vashti McKenzie wrote. And I answered that idea with another one. I wrote,

> I laugh easily and I play with abandon. The only trouble is that I often genuinely prefer to play alone. I can play a piano for hours. Or I can sit in a small boat alone till the sun goes down. Or I can read a book and never realize that I haven't seen a person for days. I enjoy a party, too—but only

some. And I love good conversation, but not always. I wonder if those things count in the "How to Be Fulfilled" exercise regimens.

The ability to be with the self is as good an indicator
as any of the ability to pray or to reflect on the things of
God or to become one with the universe. It is a sign that life
comes from within us, that we're not swallowing whole what
has been manufactured for us by someone or something else.
To be able to be in a room without the radio blaring or the
TV grinding out situation comedies gives depth to a day.

When we learn to love life more than we love loving
our pain, we become spiritually invincible. What part of life
is there that can defeat us then? There is nothing that can
take everything from us when we are openhearted enough to
love more than one thing. We see signs of that truth everywhere in holy people: a grief-stricken widow turns to paint-
ing and creates a whole new life for herself; the paraplegic
learns the computer and develops a whole new world of
friends online; the blind man who cannot see to do surgery
becomes a chiropractor with healing hands. Love of life and
love of joy are opposite sides of the same coin. When we
give ourselves to joy, we learn to love life. To love life is to
determine how to enjoy it, whatever its boundaries.

Embodied love, with all the joy and pleasure and beauty
it brings, has been made the great enemy of the spiritual life,
as if learning to be dour were a dimension of sanctity. We
were trained to beware the beautiful and the pleasurable, as if
beauty and pleasure distracted us from the God who made the
world beautiful and gave us all a capacity for pleasure.
"There's no such thing as a sad saint," the poster says. Having
come out of a Jansenist spirituality, it took me a little while
to get beyond the sourness of sin to the delight of fishing

boats and party times and wedding feasts at Cana. But I finally came to understand that there is no such thing as "loving God alone." If we love God, we love everything God made because all of them are reflections of the Love that made them.

The truth is that love makes us answerable for joy. Only selfishness gives us the right to nurse our aggravations. Love demands that it be shared and multiplied. "If there is deep love involved, there is deep responsibility toward it," May Sarton wrote. I am convinced that is right. If we really learn to love, we learn the fundamentals of the kind of joy that is more mandate than license. We learn that we have as much a responsibility to make life joyful for other people as we have a responsibility to learn to enjoy life ourselves. I wrote,

> Indeed love brings responsibility. But for what? We were trained that our responsibility was to resist love. But there is a great deal to be learned in love that can't be learned nearly as well in any other way: self-control, unselfishness, listening, care—and raw unadulterated joy. Maybe the real responsibility is to accept love—and learn.

To lust for joy is to lust for the God of life. To make joy where at first it seems there is none is to become co-creator with the God of life. When we make joy, we make a holier, happier life. The problem is that we far too often expect joy to come to us rather than realizing that we have a spiritual responsibility to make it for ourselves. So we blame God for the fact that our lives are bleak or sere or cheerless.

We make joy and comfort synonyms when, in fact, joy is not an immersion in conveniences; it is awareness of what is good even in the midst of barrenness. Some psychologists have taken to instructing depressive personalities to name three things, before going to sleep at night, that were good about the day. It could be a spiritual exercise far more im-

portant to the quality of life than an examination of conscience could ever be. An examination of conscience concentrates on everything that went wrong with the day; the
recitation of our joys concentrates on everything that makes
being alive worthwhile. If I can learn to look for joy, I might
be able to see how my own sins—my anger, my deceit, my
self-centeredness—are really the things that poison my life.
Then, I could really repent them.

The first step to being joyful is to recognize joy all
around us. "All through the long winter I dream of my garden. On the first warm day of spring I dig my fingers deep
into the soft earth . . . and my spirits soar," Helen Hayes
wrote. I could feel her words all the way through my own
body. I wrote back,

> I never dream of gardens but I do dream of keyboards and
> dogs and water. They are all the things that give me back
> myself. I sink into them and all the irritations drain away. I
> become then who I really am and I become deliriously
> happy. I become untethered from expectations and agendas
> and responsibilities. I become—I feel—truly whole. The
> spiritual discipline to be developed at a time of great pres-
> sure is to do more of the things that soak our spirits in
> laughter and smiles. But how? The dog is gone; the water is
> gone. And the keyboard intrudes on the life of others.
> However, there is always memory—and always hope.

Even in a culture as epicurean as ours, though, the old
tensions linger. We are at base a Puritan people, after all. So,
the basic question remains, Are we to enjoy this life or to
avoid it? When the world tilts to the left, religions so often tilt
to the right. Religions themselves sin against creation. They
begin to preach a spirituality of denial, rather than a spirituality of balance. They infect the world with a spirituality of

fear, rather than a spirituality of joy. They want people to give things up, rather than to learn to use them rightly. They don't admit it, but sacrifice is easier than balance.

Only the really spiritually strong know how to use a thing without abusing it; how to drink a little, but never to the point where human reason is impaired; how to take medicines without becoming drug addicts; how to distinguish between love that is sexual and sex for its own sake. And the distinctions are crucial. Joy enriches the world; self-satisfaction squeezes it dry and satiates the soul in the process. Then, jaded ourselves, we consume the resources of the other as well. Then, we turn joy into engorgement. Then, we take our fill at the price of the life of another. "Come, lure our hearts with God's desire, that we our good once more befriend," J. Mary Luti writes. She makes the point. In seeking God, we seek our real good, and what is good turns us to God. We live within the bounds of the self and in that way make joy the gift we give to others. I wrote, knowing the depth of the struggle, both in traditions of the past and in our own times as well,

> God's "desire" is a slippery thing. Does God "desire" that I enjoy life or does God want me to put all my effort into transcending it? And how do I know? Well, since I can't be sure, I have taken a new criteria for myself that comes out of the Benedictine Rule, not the catechism. The Prologue says, in essence, "Do no harm; do good." That will have to be guide enough for me right now in a culture and a church that confuse law with goodness.

To do no harm to another, to do good for everyone, makes joy a transmutable commodity. It is not an idle find, a lucky catch, a rare premium. It is a spiritual attitude of my own making.

Chapter Twenty-Five

SANCTITY:
THE TASK OF GROWING INTO GOD

We are freed by God's love to live in the freshness of each new day.

—Mary Ann Neevel

*I'm not really sure what such a sentence means. "We are freed by
God's love to live in the freshness of each new day." I'm far more inclined to think that it is in the freshness of each day that we are freed
to experience, seek, become aware of God's love. When we get stuck
in yesterday—its disappointments, its guilt—we may miss entirely
the reality of God's ever-blooming love for us. Now and here.*

—Joan Chittister, Journal, March 24

THE FIRST TIME I WENT TO ROME, EXPERIENCED THE
intrigues of the Curia, saw the politics of the system,
watched the maneuverings of national clerical alliances, and
realized how helpless women were in the face of all of it, I
felt years of ecclesiastical conditioning go to dust under my
feet. What was there left to believe in? Where was the
Shangri-la of my religious dreams? How could I possibly
continue to profess any commitment to any of this? It was
all so human. It was all so venal. It was all so depressing.

"Don't worry," the old monk said to me. "You'll be all right. Everybody who comes to Rome loses their faith here the first two weeks." Then, he smiled a small smile and added, "Then in the last two weeks, they put it back where it should have been to begin with: in Jesus."

I grew immensely in those four weeks—out of spiritual infancy into spiritual adulthood. Out of adoration of the church, into worship of the God whom this tradition had made accessible to me. To understand the value of the church, ironically, I had to understand its limitations. To worship God I had to stop worshiping the things of God. "Open yourself to the Tao," the Tao te Ching teaches, "then trust your natural responses and everything will fall into place."[9] Now I knew what that meant.

Growth in the spiritual life is a slow, circuitous route to the God within. It winds through devotion and disaster, through fidelity and sin to the point of self-knowledge and need, self-sufficiency and an unending desire for "the More."

We are steeped in God, but it takes so long to realize that the God we make in our own image is too small a God on which to waste our lives. God is the energy of the universe, the light in every soul, the eternal kaleidoscope of possibility that surrounds us in nature. The face of God is imprinted on the face of every one we see. God is no one of them, and God is more than all of them, but without them, we miss all the tiny glimpses of God we're being given on the way. "How easy it is to forget and disregard the divine beauty and light within ourselves and in the 'other,'" Deborah Chu-lan Lee wrote. It's a simple insight, but the very ground of the spiritual life, I think. I have seen God's mercy and justice, felt God's love, and heard God's voice—but always in the other. And all of them have grown me beyond myself. I wrote,

I'm not so sure that it's "easy to forget" the Divine in the other. I think, given our formation in the potential pitfalls and essential weakness of matter, that it is more likely to be impossible to see it at all. But once we do, once we realize that we are surrounded by fragments of the Divine, life becomes luminous.

Consciousness of the presence of God, once it comes, changes the way we look at the world in which we live. Then, we begin to realize the fundamental truth of life: Some things are difficult, yes, but nothing is useless. Everything we do is preparing us to embrace the God of the universe who has already absorbed us into it. Every act of ours in return is nothing more than a gesture of gratitude for the great, swirling galaxy of people and events and blessings that we know to be our lives. Then, we become part of the ongoing creation around us. Then we make our own contribution to the fullness of life. Then we grow into goodness itself.

"Every act of gratitude is incomplete," Maria Harris wrote, "unless it issues in a sending forth to do works that will make for justice." The words resounded in my own life, but I also knew the futility of them. I wrote,

"One can never pay in gratitude," Anne Morrow Lindbergh wrote. "One can only pay 'in kind' somewhere else in life." I certainly know the truth of that. So much good has been done to me, so much support given, so much money invested that there is no way for me to pay anyone back for what I myself do not have. But I can pass it on, in whatever proportion I can. I can do for others what has been done for me. I can do for others what they cannot do for themselves. I can do what must be done if everyone everywhere is also to have a good life. Then it will be enough repayment to redound through the universe forever.

The one obstacle to the worship of the God of grace, the chief barrier to gratitude, lies in a stubborn refusal to grow beyond the limits of our lives. If we were poor, or rejected, or unsuccessful yesterday, we define ourselves as unable to be anything but poor and outcast and a failure today. We refuse to claim the power within us. And we blame the rest of the world for the prisons in which we place ourselves. We smother ourselves in resentment or remorse. But to grow spiritually we must dedicate ourselves to becoming more today than we were yesterday. We must grow beyond the wounds and memories we clutch to our breasts with claw-like care, afraid that if we relax our reminiscence of them, we can no longer justify our intentions never to become more than we are. "Many of us carry around old baggage for years," Donna Schaper's excerpt read. I thought of all the things buried in me, but still burning, and I knew that she was right. I wrote,

> We all go through life at the mercy of our memories. We remember what we now miss. We remember what traumatized us and touch the scars we carry in our souls from the shock of it. I know that I often miss a sense of independence and possibility. And I always remember the glimpses of violence around me and the fear it engendered in me of so many other things. And yet, without it, would I ever have come to the spiritual life and become any kind of thinker at all? It's very doubtful. Both growth and gratitude came out of pain. Then they become the bliss of our lives.

No one goes through life unscathed. Scathing is, in fact, the process that wears away the dross of arrogance and entitlement, of preeminence and pretension. The pruning goes on all our lives until we grow into whatever shape or substance we are meant to become. We are not born whole physically. We are carried for years, nurtured for decades, educated for most of our lives. And we are not born wholly spiritual either. We wander from one god to another that we substitute for the God who is God. We learn by both the development of virtue and the degradation of sin. We come to new life by almost dying from the pain that comes with living. And in the end, we are healed by the God who always means our welfare and never our woe. "No wound is so trivial that the love of God is not concerned with it," Flora Wuellner wrote. The extract made me consider my own life, my own needs for healing across the years. I wrote,

> My healing God has always healed every wound, not by erasing it but by numbing it, by taking away its sting; not by fixing it but by providing something in its place: for a freer world, a steady one; for this community, a larger one; for one rejection or another, new welcome somewhere else of something in me that I did not myself know I had. And so my world has evolved from wound to wound. Thank the God who heals.

Life either dwarfs us or grows us. There is no in-between. There is no standing still in the spiritual life. There is only the unending opportunity to become or to die. We see people die spiritually every day. Sometimes they look very religious in the doing of it, in fact. They go on believing, reading, praying, thinking what they have always thought. In the face of new questions, they dare no questions. At the brink of new insights, they want no insights. They want comfort and a guarantee of the kind of heaven they imagined as children. They think that to think anything else is unfaithful. They believe that science is an attack on God because science cannot confirm the God they have made for themselves. And so they make something other than God their God.

But those who grow in the spiritual life know that spirituality begins where answers and pictures stop. The spiritual life is seeded in darkness and ends in light. It is about love, not law; it is about grace and energy, the cosmos and creation. It is about hope at the edge of despair and a beginning where only an end seems to be. It is about dailiness raised to the level of the ultimate assurance that God is with us. It is only up to us to be with God. "The wastelands of life around us cannot shut out the promise of life-giving water," Lavon Bayler wrote. I had a life to prove that. I wrote,

> There is that within us that shouts always, "more." As far as I'm concerned, this is our single greatest proof of the existence of God. It seems that we are born with a memory in our hearts of where we've been and consciousness of where we're going—and nothing else satisfies along the way.

Once we have come to the point that we can allow God to be for us always new, always beckoning—beyond any single way of worship, any one set of devotions, any need to be less than alive and full of the joy of it, any desire to close off people and life, any idea that the daily is dull and empty of real spiritual experience, we have begun to grow into the spiritual life. Then we are finally ready to find God in the very lives we are leading right now. No doubt about it: If we are created by God the Creator, then living creation well—in concert with creation and in communion with the Creator—is the ultimate spiritual life. Anything less than that, anything that divides life into opposing parts—into the "spiritual" and the "material"—as if one were not the essence of the other, may be religion, but how can it possibly be a healthy spirituality? That, without doubt, must be questioned.

Epilogue

THIS BOOK DOES NOT PRETEND TO ADDRESS ALL THE issues in the spiritual life. I'm not even sure what all of those might be. This book deals only with those issues that emerged in my own life over a period of four years.

Even those it does not deal with definitively. If I addressed these same questions today, I might answer differently. I might answer in greater depth. I might answer with less passion—or with more.

So what is the purpose of a book such as this? Perhaps only to demonstrate that we all change and struggle and develop as we go. The notion that the spiritual life is something we achieve gets little support here. The spiritual life is something we seek every day of our lives. It involves a journey of ever-increasing depth and circularity. We don't deal with major questions once. We deal with them over and over again, each time—if we're lucky—understanding them differently, learning from them more, dealing with them better, until our vision of them clears and our hearts calm.

If this book is worth anything to anyone at all, it may simply be that it indicates that life, even the spiritual life, is not over until it's over. And that growing is both the same, and distinct, for all of us. Whatever the dark uncertainty of the spiritual journey, the sometimes barbed unquiet that comes with real questions, may you carry within you without fail the promise of the One who says, "Seek and you shall find."

NOTES

1. Peter Lorie and Manuela Dunn Mascetti, eds. *The Quotable Spirit: A Treasury of Religious Spiritual Quotations from Ancient Times to the Twentieth Century* (Edison, N.J.: Castle Books, 2000), 145.

2. Stephen Mitchell, *Tao te Ching* (New York: Harper Perennial, 1992), 6.

3. Lorie and Mascetti, *The Quotable Spirit*, 181.

4. Leo Rosten, *Leo Rosten's Treasury of Jewish Quotations* (New York: Bantam Books, 1972), 222.

5. Fidelis Morgan, *A Misogynist's Source Book* (London: Jonathan Cape, 1990), 183.

6. Gordon Mursell, ed., *The Story of Christian Spirituality: Two Thousand Years, from East to West* (Minneapolis: Fortress Press, 2001), 227.

7. Thorstein Veblen, "Theory of the Leisure Class," American studies at the University of Virginia, at http://xroads.virginia.edu/~HYPER/VEBLEN/chap04.html, accessed September 15, 2003.

8. Nikki Katz, "Gender Stereotypes—What You Need to Know about Gender Stereotypes," at http://womensissues. about/com/cs/genderstereotypes/a/aagenderstereo.htm, accessed September 15, 2003.

9. Mitchell, *Tao te Ching*, 23.

ABOUT THE AUTHOR

Joan D. Chittister, OSB, has been a leading voice in contemporary spirituality and church and world issues for over twenty-five years. A widely-published author, columnist, and noted international lecturer, Sr. Joan is the author of over twenty-five books, is a regular columnist for the *National Catholic Reporter* and has published numerous articles on issues involving women in church and society, human rights, peace and justice, the Catholic Church, and contemporary religious life. Her most recent book, *Scarred by Struggle, Transformed by Hope*, was named Best General Interest Book for 2003 from the Association of Theological Booksellers.

She is presently serving as co-chair of the Global Peace Initiative of Women Religious and Spiritual Leaders, a group that formed from the Fourth UN Conference of Women in Beijing to facilitate peace efforts between women, especially in the Middle East. She is also a founding member of the International Committee for the Peace Council, an interreligious group of leaders working for peace.

Sr. Joan is past president of the Leadership Conference of Women Religious, the organization of leaders of

Catholic religious women in the United States. She served as prioress of her own community, the Benedictine Sisters of Erie, Pennsylvania for twelve years.

Sister Joan is the executive director of Benetvision: a resource and research center for contemporary spirituality in Erie, Pennsylvania. Recipient of eleven honorary doctorates, she received her Ph.D. in communications theory from Penn State University.